T0084707

Tradition as Challenge

Josef Pieper Works from St. Augustine's Press

The Christian Idea of Man
Preface by John Haldane; trans. Dan Farrelly

The Concept of Sin
Trans. Edward A. Oaks, S.J.

Death and Immortality
Trans. Richard and Clara Winston

Enthusiasm and Divine Madness: On the Platonic Dialogue Phaedrus
Trans. Richard and Clara Winston

Happiness and Contemplation
Introduction by Ralph McInerny; trans. Richard and Clara Winston

In Tune with the World: A Theory of Festivity
Trans. Richard and Clara Winston

Not Yet the Twilight (vol. II of Pieper's autobiography)
Trans. Dan and Una Farrelly

The Platonic Myths
Introduction by James V. Schall; trans. Dan Farrelly

Scholasticism: Problems and Personalities of Medieval Philosophy
Trans. Richard and Clara Winston

The Silence of Goethe
Preface by Ralph McInerny; trans. Dan Farrelly

The Silence of St. Thomas: Three Essays
Trans. John Murray, S.J., and Danial O'Connor

Tradition: Concept and Claim
Trans. E. Christian Kopff

What Catholics Believe (with Heinz Raskop)
Introduction by Gerald B. Phelan; trans. Christopher Huntington

What Does "Academic" Mean?
Trans. Dan Farrelly

The Story – Where Will It End? (vol. III of Pieper's autobiography)
Trans. Dan and Una Farrelly

Don't Worry about Socrates: Three Plays for Television
Trans. Dan Farrelly

Rules of the Game in Social Relationships
Trans. Dan Farrelly

Tradition as Challenge

Essays and Speeches

JOSEF PIEPER

Translation by Dan Farrelly

ST. AUGUSTINE'S PRESS
South Bend, Indiana

Translation copyright © 2015 by St. Augustine's Press
Originally published as *Tradition als Herausforderung: Aufsätze
und Reden* by Kösel-Verlag, Munich, Germany

All rights reserved. No part of this book may be reproduced,
stored in a retrieval system, or transmitted, in any form
or by any means, electronic, mechanical, photocopying,
recording, or otherwise, without the prior permission of
St. Augustine's Press.

Manufactured in the United States of America

1 2 3 4 5 6   20 19 18 17 16 15

Library of Congress Cataloging in Publication Data
Pieper, Josef, 1904–1997.
[Tradition als Herausforderung. English]
Tradition as challenge: essays and speeches / Josef Pieper;
translation by Dan Farrelly. – 1st [edition].
pages cm
Includes bibliographical references (pages   ) and index.
ISBN 978-1-58731-882-5 (clothbound: alk. paper) –
ISBN 978-1-58731-883-2 (paperbound: alk. paper)
1. Philosophy. I. Farrelly, Daniel J., 1934– II. Title.
B29.P53713 2013
193 – dc23   2012039821

∞ The paper used in this publication meets the minimum re-
quirements of the American National Standard for Information
Sciences Permanence of Paper for Printed Materials,
ANSI Z39.481984.

ST. AUGUSTINE'S PRESS
www.staugustine.net

"Freedom acquired by the devious ploy of forgetting is empty."

WJATSCHESLAW IWANOW

Contents

Contents

ix

Tradition in the Changing World

The observation that we live in a constantly changing world is not exactly original. One will hardly read or hear any reflections on the present age that do not discuss this point – and rightly so. Of course, the focus is mainly on changes which man himself brings about, above all, progress in technical mastery over nature and her energies. And one can again and again be astonished by the extent to which, in this field, also the tempo of change is constantly intensified. A modern "Monk of Heisterbach" would not need to sleep through a century, nor even a generation, but only five years, and he would, in waking up, only half understand the daily talk – precisely the "talk of the day" – because, for example, he would not yet have heard about artificial earth satellites and planets. It seems to be no different in the realm of pure science. A university colleague said to me recently, perhaps exaggerating slightly: if his own teachers were today to visit his lectures on mathematics they would scarcely be able to follow him.

However, these changes which we have brought about ourselves in no way account for the whole world of change in which we are living today. There is even good reason for saying that the really decisive changes that define our history are of a quite different kind. The more decisive ones are perhaps those which, unlike the technical advances, happen to us – which does not have to mean that they come about without any contribution on our part. Naturally, we should also not think of these changes as if, through them, the essence, the nature of *homo sapiens*, is affected and altered by them. What I mean, rather, is change in the mode of existence, in the

1

structure, in the inner style and in the atmosphere of moral life, i.e. of the actions for which man himself is responsible – above all, of the communal life of men as they live together.

By chance, as I was recently paging through Goethe's autobiographical writings, I came across what is perhaps not a particularly significant but is both a characteristic and amusing example of such change. It occurs in the *Kampagne in Frankreich* – in the records of the strange campaign, which foundered miserably in mud and rain, of the European monarchical forces pitted against the people's army of the French Revolution. In this war, which in many ways really belongs to our era, an arrangement was still able to be made between the warring armies: the outposts on both sides, when the weather was bad (in September! in France!) had the right, depending on the direction of the wind, wrapped in their overcoats, to turn their backs to the enemy without this temporary defenselessness being exploited. We find this entry in Goethe's diary for 24 September 1792. There is no need to stress how unimaginable such a thing has become for those who lived during the last World War. This individual anecdote is, of course, quite unimportant. But what unspoken (because taken for granted and not considered worth mentioning) presuppositions of a quite general nature are contained in such an agreement; what measure, for example, of trusting humanity, what complete absence of ideological incitement and humorlessness! So, in this respect something has obviously changed in the meantime – in ourselves and with ourselves.

But it is not my intention to over-interpret a fortuitous example and, on that basis, to start singing a hymn of praise of times gone by. I am very well aware of the horrible murders of one and a half thousand innocent people, which a demagogical people's tribune could mobilize the population of Paris to carry out – in that same month of September 1792. Of course, it must immediately be added that even these horrors (at that time the very modern word "terror" found its way into the human language with this specific meaning) – even the *régime de la Terreur* was only child's play in comparison with the systematic inhumanity that took place under the brutal regimes of our present epoch. I shall not be drawn into the question whether the "human race" (as Immanuel Kant expressed it, incidentally, in an essay that bears the date 1792) is continually regressing to the bad or whether, despite everything, is constantly moving forward and improving. We know that Kant himself supported the thesis – or more precisely, the hypothesis – of progress. We can now let this matter rest. What I am concerned with is to show that the changes which are entwined in the many-stranded web of our historical development are of very different kinds.

Two of these strands, above all, can be distinguished from one another with a certain degree of clarity. The first strand consists of the changes in the sphere of scientific exploration of the world and – based on this – of the technical control and exploitation of natural energies: from the primitive tools of prehistoric man up to the modern atomic reactor. These changes, it seems to me, take a clearly discernible direction, and their law can be quite unambiguously formulated with the words: development, perfection, advance, "progress." Occasional detours and cul-de-sacs do not alter the main phenomenon: that what follows in the future, once it has been

3

accepted, is the higher stage, and that in every innovation – on the whole – what is more correct and better gets its chance.

Something completely different from these are the changes which, like the example from Goethe's *Kampagne in Frankreich*, directly concern the sphere of spiritual and moral existence, both of the individual and of society. Here it is clearly not possible to say, for instance, that every factual innovation is *eo ipso* an improvement. And the direction this change takes is not at all, of itself, a necessarily positive one. Progress, advance, perfection are quite possible; but the realization of this possibility can in no way be taken for granted. Human freedom is at play here in a unique way; and man is challenged, both in his individual and in his social existence, to make a quite specific effort. What is right does not come about "of itself." One could almost say: on the contrary, that what comes about when we let things take their course is what is false and bad! Of course, neither does scientific and technical progress happen of itself – without the most intense human application. But there is an essential difference. In the scientific and technical realm there is such a thing as an objective dynamic, intrinsic to the things themselves, which is sometimes achieved over the heads of the scholars and independently of them. A modern physicist has said: "The law of gravity and the spectral splitting up of light could not have remained undiscovered, even without Newton. It would have only taken longer"; something similar can be said of the discoveries by Hertz and Einstein. "It would have taken longer." Yes, the slowing down of progress can happen in this sphere, even a standstill, but not a wrong development or a degeneration. Yet these are very much possible in the realm of spiritual and moral existence, not only with regard to the individual but also with regard to society – for which reason changes such as take place here are a matter of grave concern to those for whom responsibility for mankind has some meaning. Also the deep feeling of worry which, as everyone knows, is bound up with the sudden availability of atomic energy, is related, strictly speaking, not at all to this scientific and technical achievement as such – which, of course, remains an undoubtedly magnificent thing. But, naturally, exploration of the world and subjugation of nature are not something that can be isolated from human existence as a whole. And here is the subject of concern: whether man, as a spiritual and moral being, can be trusted or reasonably expected not to make wrong use of the scientific and technical achievement through which monstrous power is delivered into his hands.

A large part of that worry about what man might become, in the midst of this world which is changing ever faster and more fundamentally, has been concerned with the preservation of something that remains constant throughout all the turbulent change; of course, not just *something or other* that remains; it is, instead, a question of keeping pure and unadulterated the truly human possession, that original gift of truth about man himself and about the world; it is a question of preserving the inheritance from which man – not just the man of knowledge, but also the man of action – is nourished and which is the foundation of his life. That this *thesaurus* should not be lost in oblivion but handed down intact through the generations and received by them – then handed down further and again received – that is what is important. To say it differently: the worry, arising from the vehement historical changes, about what makes up the truly human – this worry is growing with similar intensity and has become identical with the worry about *tradition*.

In the exact moment that I utter this word "tradition," a choir of many critical voices, composed of alarm, defense, opposition, and protest makes itself heard. Everyone knows to what extent terms denoting "tradition" are encumbered with more or less vague negative value judgments originating from both emotional and ideological sources. And anyone familiar with the history of ideas is quite aware how much argument and difference of opinion has been kindled, ever anew, precisely by the concept and the claims of tradition. How often have historical forces, now suffering from loss of impact and from exhaustion, appealed to "tradition," to what has been thought, said, and done from "time immemorial." And have not the great things of our own era come about despite the tough resistance of what is purely traditional? "Progress" clearly says, above all: away from what has been, and move on to what has never been before. And, in the end, what harm would be done if a new generation simply ignored tradition, to think, say, and do something radically new? And finally, how can the claim be identified that sees itself as necessarily behind all tradition and without which tradition is not thinkable?

These critical objections and questions, which in today's world largely characterize the intellectual, are not to be taken lightly. And no one who undertakes to defend the claim of tradition and to show it as a necessary element of a complete, rounded, and meaningful human existence can dispense himself from becoming involved with this opposing position.

The first thing that must happen is to achieve the greatest possible conceptual clarity. It is above all necessary to situate the concept of "tradition" in its right and proper place. The difference of opinion (referred to) seems to originate, in no small measure – in the past and today – from the fact that the appeal to tradition has happened, and does happen, in the wrong place: for example (again!), in the sphere of the scientific exploration of the world and in the practical sphere which is based on it. It is not by chance that the first fundamental discussion about the binding nature of tradition in general was kindled precisely here. I am referring to the very dramatic debate about "empty space" in which such outstanding minds as Galileo, Descartes, and Pascal took part. Central to this debate was the dogma, in natural philosophy, of the *horror vacui* – handed down from antiquity and the Middle Ages – according to which nature abhors a vacuum, and that therefore there is no such thing. The contribution to this discussion by scholars in natural science at that time has gone down in the history of science under the name of the Torricellian vacuum. It is the determined attempt to create, through experiment, the empty space which seemed metaphysically impossible. The details of this debate, which was carried out with extraordinary passion, are of no further interest here. What is important, however, is the very clear thesis about tradition which Pascal, at the age of twenty-four, distilled for himself out of the experience of this methodological debate. Put in a somewhat simplified and brief formulation, Pascal's conclusion is as follows: obviously there are two different types of scientific study. Those of the first type are based on experience and arguments from reason, the model of this type being physics. Those of the

7

second type are based on authority and tradition, the model of this type being theology. In the sphere of empirical sciences there is no point in appealing to authority and tradition. "The ancients say . . . ," "Aristotle teaches . . . ," "according to custom handed down one acts in this way . . . ," "traditionally this or that is the accepted thing . . ." – it is not possible to argue in this way in physics or in any other empirical science. "The ancients" (says Pascal) – that is ourselves rather than Aristotle, who, compared with us, was young and inexperienced. It is certainly true, Pascal continues, that it is one of the "confusions" of his own century to declare innovations in physics to be false purely because they do not agree with the opinion of the ancients and with tradition. The same had already been said, by the way, four hundred years before Pascal – by Albertus Magnus. If I want to know whether a dolphin is a fish or a mammal, then (says Albert) I do not look up Aristotle, but I ask those who have experience in this matter: *experimentum solum certificat in talibus*: "experience alone gives certainty in such things"; "there is no philosophy about the concrete." For the thirteenth century these are astounding and daring statements, with which, of course, Albertus Magnus was at that time still not able to achieve much. In the meantime, what he said has become more or less taken for granted, namely, that, wherever it is a question of truths which can be grasped by means of experience and reason, an appeal to tradition is simply no argument – whether it is tradition founded on the Bible or on Aristotle. Certainly at this point it should be added: or on Karl Marx! For also this appeal to the authority of an author who is declared canonical has formally the structure and character of "tradition." And as a scientific

8

argument it has just as little weight as an appeal to the authority of Aristotle. And, besides, exactly like the most obdurate conservatism of the Aristotelians in late scholasticism, it hinders scientific progress; and, yet again, it brings true and legitimate tradition into undeserved disrepute.

But, of course, even in its own specific field, tradition can in many different ways be robbed of respect and effectiveness; it can be endangered or simply destroyed. To see this more clearly, one must try to grasp more precisely what is really meant by the concept of "tradition." In normal parlance it always has two meanings: on the one hand, the process of handing on, *tradere*, and, on the other hand, the content of what is handed on: the *traditum* or the *tradendum*.

Tradition as an historical process takes place between two partners, an older and a younger one, a father and a son, between two generations. To be precise, it is not a dialogue, not an exchange, not a mutual communication but, so to speak, a "one-way" communication. One partner, the one handing on, speaks, and the other listens – when and insofar as it is a question of the tradition process. And naturally, between the generations that follow one another other things are at work apart from tradition (in the strict sense); when things run properly there is, for example, conversation between the old and the young, back and forth, from which both sides profit. It is, furthermore, important that the one handing on in the tradition process does not hand down anything of his own, anything he has acquired himself, but something that he, too, has received from elsewhere. To this again it has to be said that, naturally, in the relationship between the generations there is also a handing on of what one has acquired oneself – for instance, in the case of the researcher who, by teaching, communicates his own discoveries. But we do not call this "tradition" in the strict sense. Language itself resists this use of the term. Tradition, therefore, does not simply mean handing on something, but rather, handing on something which has already been received as handed on. *Quod a patribus acceperunt, hoc filiis tradiderunt*; what has been received from one's fathers is passed on to the sons. This sentence from Augustine designates the structure of the process with complete precision.

But now we have to speak of another element of this process. It is the decisive element and at the same time the critical point about the process of tradition. I am referring to the reception of the *tradendum* x – what is to be passed on – by the "last in the series," the young generation. This is immediately apparent: if the "last in the series" does not receive, does not accept what is offered him in this process (with a view to his passing it on), then tradition does not come about; it does not happen at all. That is why I said this is the critical, the sensitive spot.

The first question to ask is: of what kind is this reception, what does it look like, how does it happen? Second, what are the presuppositions for its coming about? Receiving the *tradendum* does not happen simply through taking cognizance of it. It is possible for me to know it very well and still not accept it. Here there is a problem which is very relevant today which I can here only point out. It is the problem of history and tradition: namely, that, despite the most extensive historical knowledge of the material of tradition, it is nevertheless possible to be without tradition, because – to use Gabriel Marcel's words – what happens is merely a registering, but there is no longer any memory. Taking notice and having knowledge is clearly, on the part of the receiver, not enough for tradition – as a process of handing on – to come about and be completed. Instead, what is required is that the one who is "last in the series" accepts the *tradendum* really *as* something handed on to him and therefore as something he does not already have and does not take himself, but as something he allows himself to be given by another and for which only someone else provides the guarantee. That means that it is required that he accept the *tradendum* as valid and affirm it on the authority of another – without the possibility of his examining it and verifying it for himself. In other words, if it is at all possible to speak of "tradition" in the strict sense of the word, something is presupposed on the part of the receiver which corresponds fairly exactly to what people call "faith." We hardly need specially to mention why the coming into being of this act of faith is bound up with manifold conditions and that there are as many (concomitant) difficulties, dangers, and obstacles.

One such obstacle which is continually set up by the older generation, i.e., by the generation that at any given time in history has its hand on the tiller, is precisely the use of the name "tradition". It is hardly possible to undertake anything more hopeless than to say to a young person, in answer to his critical question why and on what basis something handed down should continue to be accepted, that it is "tradition." This argument, which, incidentally, does not have to be expressly formulated, not only does not find acceptance but hinders the young person, for his part, from achieving any living realization of the *traditum*. Besides, such an answer shows that the older generation no longer manages to make of the tradition a living presence in their own lives and that here we are already facing what has been called "bad preservation" (of tradition). In last year's festivals in the Ruhr it was said, in public discussion, that tradition disappears as soon as it is mentioned by name; that precisely this explicit mention destroys it. Of course, that is an extreme formulation, but it makes an important point. Whoever wants to hand on tradition must see that the content of the tradition, the "old truths," are kept really alive – for example, through a living language, through creative rejuvenation and the shedding of skins, so to speak, through continual confrontation with the immediately present, and, above all, with the future, since in the human sphere that alone is the truly real. It can be seen here, first, what an ambitious task is included in the act of handing on. According to a Hebrew saying: "teaching old things is harder than teaching new things." But what comes to light here is how wrong it is to associate the concept of "tradition" with the idea of being static, of persisting, or even of stagnating. Tradition, as the living process of handing on, is a highly dynamic thing, so that real consciousness of tradition has only little to do with "conservatism." There is no doubt that there are forms of conservatism which, on the contrary, actually hinder tradition – because they cling to the chance external form in which the *tradendum* appears in history, whereas it can only, if at all, be passed on to the future under *new* external forms. On the other hand, there is undoubtedly a real passing down in the true and finest sense, of which undiscriminating, fundamental conservatism of the so-called "cult of tradition" variety is not aware – precisely because the *traditum* is presented and received in a changed historical form. But this is ultimately the crucial point: that the content and substance, which transcends time, is preserved down through the generations.

Well, then, one may perhaps say, what is this content, for the sake of which the effort of keeping it alive is worthwhile? One only needs to look around and it is clear that the content of tradition can cover the whole range of historical reality and belong to every sphere of human existence. An institution, a song, a legal text, a wedding or funeral custom, but also a teaching, a statement about reality and existence – all can be handed down. There are traditional times for meals and traditional foods; feasts, costumes, sayings, gestures. All of these can be characterized as handed down. The radius of what can be handed down stretches from the outermost periphery of behaviour, from the way we put food into our mouths, the way we offer and receive a greeting, the way we keep animals – right to the kernel of religious conviction and ritual.

Periphery and kernel – that, of course, is the vital distinction on which everything depends. And yet it has its own vagaries. We celebrate "in a traditional way" a birthday and a shooting festival; and it is likewise "tradition" that Easter is celebrated, as is the first day of the week. Here it is quite obvious that the content of these traditions has varying significance and that the traditions themselves are highly distinct with regard to their binding force. A birthday or a shooting festival, if the time happens not to be right, can be omitted without qualms; but, not to celebrate Easter – that is clearly something of an entirely different order! That does not at all mean that the less important celebrations have no meaning and could be cut away. It could well be that a group of people who are discarding their costume or ceasing to bake their

13

bread or cakes in a particular form begin, at the same moment, also to lose the traditions which directly concern the centre of their existence. However, we will not justifiably speak of "loss of tradition," "break with tradition," or "lack of tradition" if the external trappings of historical life alter their traditional shape. These terms, which we are perhaps too ready to use, should be saved up for the case where the innermost, middle strand of the link with tradition is severed.

However, if one is looking for a distinctive characteristic, a common feature that distinguishes the *tradita* which have the highest claim on our commitment, one will find that the characteristic common to them all is "sacred tradition" – and it does not matter whether we are dealing with moral norms for living, with interpretation of the meaning of the world and existence, with the celebration of the great feasts, or with the substance of artistic representation. With regard to this last point one might call to mind the statement made by Goethe in later life: "Every genuine artist is to be seen as one who wants to preserve what is acknowledged as sacred and to propagate it with seriousness and careful consideration. But every century strives, in its own way, to be part of the secular, and seeks to make the sacred ordinary, the heavy light, and the serious funny. Nothing need be said against this as long as the result is not to destroy both the serious and the funny."

But when we ask the great Athenian who, in Western Europe, stimulates philosophical interpretation of existence right down to the present day and keeps it in suspense – if we ask Plato what, in his opinion, is the quintessence of the "wisdom of the ancients," this is the answer we receive: that the world proceeded from the ungrudging goodness of God; that God holds in his hands the beginning, the middle, and the end of all things; that the soul of man survives death; that it is worse to do injustice than to suffer it; that, after death, judgment awaits us, along with punishment and reward, and so on. One can see immediately that here Plato is speaking of nothing other than the divine guarantee that the world has meaning and that man is safe. And so it is the same theme spoken about in the Christian tradition – although in a completely new way. And yet I think it important to describe the mythical tradition that Plato conjures up of the pre-Christian and non-Christian world. I want to make clear how much the human race, throughout all historical ages and in the whole compass of its cultural variations, is – beyond all expectations – of one mind precisely in relation to *sacred tradition*. One could almost dare to maintain that this sacred tradition, which is everywhere fundamentally identical, actually constitutes the spiritual unity of the human race.

But we are still trying to answer the question: what is there, amid the crowded diversity of the factual material handed down, that needs – as such and indisputably, despite all change – to be preserved as essential: as essential because otherwise the continuity of what is truly human would be destroyed? It is a question of what content of tradition has the absolute claim to be kept alive at all times so that each new generation is in a position – and thus can be expected – to accept and affirm it with full and fresh energy. The answer to this question will again be: they are the aspects of tradition which can be referred to as sacred tradition; they are what, in truth, is worth preserving and what it is necessary to preserve. As I already said, wherever there is the will to hand on tradition of this kind it will give freedom and, at the same time, independence over against the timid rigidity of the mere forms of conservatism. And whoever takes on the real task of handing on tradition will soon become aware that, much as tradition implies preservation, it deals primarily not with conserving but much more with enlivening, imposing a new shape, finding a new formulation – something which cannot be achieved without direct involvement in the current problems of the age.

Of course, one must be prepared to face the last of the critical objections we have spoken about. We are still involved in debate with a partner who denies tradition. But this partner is in no way a fiction. On the contrary, we will find that, in any public discussion, he represents the majority. Nietzsche was correct in his diagnosis: "What is most under attack today is the instinct and will for tradition; all institutions which owe their origin to this instinct are in confrontation with the taste of the modern mind." Naturally, this diagnosis is not an argument which could counter any objection. – The objection is as follows: sacred tradition and wisdom of the ancients are big words; but they are only words. "Sacred" is what demands reverence and respect of everyone. But on what basis is that which is called sacred tradition really supposed to be binding on us? Why "must" it absolutely be preserved and handed on? How can such an obligation be substantiated? "Continuity of the truly human"? All very fine, but where is it written that humanity is not perhaps in the process of fundamental change? And who are "the ancients," in fact? How is the authority attributed to them to be legitimized?

Again, Plato has given an answer to this last question which, to my mind, has timeless validity. There is, as is

16

well known, frequent mention in the Platonic dialogues of "the ancients," the *palaioí* and *archaíoi*. A name is never mentioned. "The ancients" remain anonymous; but we are not dealing here with a vague notion. From the very meaning of the term it is clear, for example, that reference is not being made to old men, those advanced in years, those who have become wise through having lived a long life, but to those who were close to the origin, the early ones, the ones at the beginning. The ancients are the first link in the chain on which everything that follows remains dependent. They are, however, completely different from the "pioneers" who broke new ground in the field of empirical science. Undoubtedly, the memory of these, too, is honored, and they are commemorated with gratitude and respect whenever a jubilee is to be celebrated. But they are "outdated" – by the very progress which they themselves initiated. What they have to say is only "historically" interesting. By contrast, "the wisdom of the ancients" has an inexhaustible relevance to the present. One could say that the ancients occupy, in the sphere where tradition applies, the place that is due, in the sphere of the empirical sciences, to the men who have produced the newest and latest findings. This ranking of "the ancients" is based, as Plato expressed it, on the fact that, "settling close to the gods," they were the first to receive knowledge which has come down from a supra-human source, a *theios logos*, a divine saying, and that, since then, anyone who wants to share this message – which is not accessible to man in a natural way – is dependent on them. In brief: the ultimate legitimation of the "wisdom of the ancients" and of the sacred tradition incorporated in it is, according to Plato, revelation and inspiration in the strict sense; these alone provide the foundation for the obligatory nature of tradition insofar as it is binding on man.

Naturally, "revelation" and "inspiration" are words which only have their full and exact meaning in the context of Christian theology, and it is obvious that this meaning is not precisely formulated in the Platonic dialogues and is not to be found there. But the decisive common element is absolutely clear; and, incidentally, it links, to my mind, Christian teaching not just with the philosophy of the Greeks but also with the originally mythical wisdom of all peoples and cultures. Without exception they say that the kernel of every tradition is always sacred tradition – from which the accompanying external traditions growing up around it derive their meaning and, even when this has died away or been abandoned, can achieve new growth. But this kernel is "sacred" (and that means also: commanding unconditional reverence) by virtue of taking its origin from a "Divine" utterance – however this may have been heard. This is the ultimate, and, when it comes down to it, the sole sufficient reason why something that has come down to us through the ages must continue to be preserved intact and handed on from generation to generation.

Only such a radical answer can also – if at all –respond satisfactorily to the equally fundamental question which concerns not just this or that tradition, but tradition as such. But if this radical answer cannot be managed, i.e. if it can neither be given nor accepted, at that moment there is no longer any prospect of doing anything to counter the acute danger of a total loss of tradition. And it would be difficult to say how the destruction of its substance could be halted – the substance from which not only the individual but also society lives.

It is possible, finally, that a terrifying and hence salutary experience could be productive – one of which anyone in this era must have had an inkling or some awareness. The poet-philosopher Wjatscheslaw Iwanow, who was a pupil of Solowjew and who died in Rome in 1949, wrote with validity about this experience in a strange little book which has the odd title: *Correspondence Between Two Corners of the Room*. What at first may sound like an idyll in the manner of Andersen's fairy tales is a to some extent dangerous discussion between the Christian Iwanow and the liberal historian Michael Gerschenson – dangerous because it takes place in Bolshevik Russia, where these two find themselves for a while put into the same room of a state rest home for intellectual workers. Gerschenson makes the case for simply casting off the burden of tradition and making a tabula rasa: "What a great thing it would be to dive into the river of Lethe to wash away, without trace, all memory of religion, philosophy, art, and poetry, and to set foot on the shore like the first man, naked, light and joyful." Against this, Iwanow defends the healing power of tradition, which he calls "eternal memory"; he celebrates it as "the life blood of all society based on spirit" and as the only force which reunites us with the origin and with the word which was there in the beginning.

The shallow fruit of conscious lack of tradition, that terrifying experience I referred to, Iwanow formulated in a superb sentence: "Freedom acquired by the devious ploy of forgetting is empty."

What Is Meant by the "Christian West"?

What particularly characterizes the "Christian West" is a question that has often been raised, discussed, and answered in recent years. Whoever undertakes to introduce the discussion anew must be prepared to face doubt whether an answer can be expected that is binding and goes beyond purely rhetorical programming of culture. The following essay is based on the conviction that such an answer is, indeed, not only possible but that it must always be provided insofar as our self-understanding is important to us.

What, then, is meant by "Christian West"? To begin with, the counter question might come to mind: is there such a thing as a non-Christian West? Can we manage to conceive of the "West" deliberately leaving out "Christian" or even thinking deliberately of a positively non-Christian culture? That is, of course, purely a question of fact, a question of history. By "history" is not meant, on the other hand, merely the objectively observed thing of the past but also the present and the future. And in this sphere of current reality even questions of fact challenge us to make a decision about what will be fact – how future reality is to look.

Just how much our notion is affected by what ought to be; how much we are "involved" when there is discussion about the West and about Western culture; how important are the imponderables of these concepts (by which is meant anything but diffuse sorts of feelings but rather conceptual elements which are difficult to put into clear words; precisely *that* is one of the reasons why the question repeatedly becomes an earnest one: what is meant by the West?) – how impossible it is to dispatch this question with quick, deft answers can be seen, for example, when in discussions with Anglo-Saxons "Western culture" unceremoniously and suddenly becomes "Western civilization." I have always felt a little as if my words were being twisted in my mouth and as if the best and most important part of my meaning was, by some trick, knocked out of my hand – and this, despite the fact that, on the other hand, I felt it was both beneficial and at first painful, to expose my German thought to the test of genuineness and simplicity by having it translated into the ruthless sobriety of the English language. Thus it is undoubtedly quite healthy to have it pointed out that "West" (Abend) here simply means where the sun goes down, namely, the west.

But, in all seriousness, there is no need to explain that the "West" was originally a place designation and one thought of as inner-European. But even this is not as unambiguous as one perhaps might think. What is the East that is opposite this "West"? For the Greeks, for the contemporaries of Aristotle, the "East" was the Middle East, Persia, the Asia opened up by Alexander – at the same time it might be asked whether Greece itself was not considered to be "West." For Augustine, Ambrose, and Boethius the East is Byzantium, Rome of the East. And this casting off, this achieving of independence by the Latin half of the Empire over against the Greek-speaking half – becoming aggravated and deepened when, in the eleventh century, the Eastern Church broke away from the Roman Church – this has very much to do with what must be called the origin of the West. Not that this separated West is simply "the West"! For the Greeks the "East" was the Middle East. But the people of the Old Testament belonged to the Middle East! And who could think of the "West" without the biblical story of creation, without the Book of Job, without the Psalms? The separation of the Latin West from the Greek East had to do with the origin of the "West," as I said; yet Greek civilization – Plato, Aristotle, Neoplatonism (the Syrian Christian – still a puzzle – who wrote under the name of Dionysius Areopagita near the beginning of the sixth century was translated by Irishmen and Franconians from Greek into Western languages, and, thanks to their translations, this Neoplatonic mystic is one of the most powerful authorities at the University of Paris throughout the whole medieval period) – all of this is part of the substance of the "West," not to speak of the Greek Fathers of Christendom: Origen, Athanasius, Chrysostom!

It is clear that this question is extremely complicated, when, despite all that has been said, it still must be admitted that it is the West, the Western mentality that makes all this material into what we call, down to this day, "Western culture." – The West: that is, of course, not just the Latin, the West-Roman. It includes the young peoples [Völker. DF] who penetrated into the West-Roman Empire from the north and then very soon learnt its language: Latin. It is, for example, above all the Goths for whom Boethius undertakes to translate the Greek philosophers – into Latin, it should be noted.

Now we need to treat of the substance, the content of this Latin, Western – and now we can and must add – Germanic mind. And this would be the starting point for the proper answer to the question: "What is meant by the 'Christian West'?" – the attempt at an answer, the suggestion to look at and consider a definite answer.

The answer can be compressed into these few words:

theologically grounded existence in the world! This is meant as the quintessence and the distinctive character of the Western mind.

One thing is immediately clear: if this is so, the West is by its very nature, and from the beginning, a tense arrangement. It is an explosive combination and it undoubtedly requires a special intellectual and spiritual energy to link both elements – and to keep them linked – so that neither of them grows out of control and that neither causes the disappearance of the other. Existence in the world has, of itself, the natural tendency to separate itself from its foundation in theology and religion. And religion is always tempted to become unworldly. To think both elements together, and, above all, to live them together: that is the "Christian West"! This is what distinguishes it from the non-Western and also from a non-Western Christianity!

But now we must say more precisely what is meant by this concept of a theologically grounded existence in the world! It means, first, an affirming attitude towards the world. "World" means here, above all, the visible world, the world of the things we can see, hear, smell, taste, and touch. It includes also the affirmation of real living humanity itself, and, not least, the affirmation and recognition of natural human reason! Existence in the world, therefore, amounts to taking seriously natural reality in all its aspects. This natural reality possesses, it is maintained, a genuine being and function of its own, which cannot be ignored and obliterated by any kind of absolutizing of the "religious."

In the first thousand years of Christendom such a positive attitude to the world was not at all taken for granted. And yet this attitude – despite all appearances –

is aware of having Christian and biblical legitimation. Of course it is an extraordinary novelty that the Roman Boethius, around the year 500, writes a tract about the divine Trinity in which there is not one single quotation from the Bible. And yet the monks of the Norman Benedictine Abbey Le Bec are on the same track when, 500 years later, they ask their Abbot to write a theodicy in which everything is based on reason and nothing on the authority of Sacred Scripture. The astounding thing is that these are monks, Benedictines living in strict isolation from the world, who express such demands and that it is a saint who fulfills this wish; it is none other than the Lombard Anselm, who later as Archbishop of Canterbury becomes Primate of England.

What begins with Boethius and Anselm finds its fully developed form in the thirteenth century: more precisely, in what is called the Aristotle reception. It is the extraordinarily dynamic process in which the enormous stock of knowledge of the world and of world wisdom, which suddenly became known to Christendom in the work of Aristotle, is subsumed into the Christian theological interpretation of the world. Managing this assimilation is the achievement of the Swabian Albertus Magnus and his Hohenstaufen pupil from Southern Italy, Thomas Aquinas.

At the same time Thomas also gave the theological justification for this seemingly so dangerous attitude to the world its first formulation. Incidentally, it had not only the appearance of danger, but it was, as Thomas clearly saw, a very real danger. But Thomas also saw that this Aristotelian affirmation of the visible world was not at all foreign and "heathen"; he recognized this openness to the world, and saw it as something originally

Christian. He laid claim to it, at first in the face of opposition from the then dominant theology, as Christian property.

This claim is based, above all, on two theological arguments. In this the second element of the Western mentality is expressed, since existence in the world is not enough, of itself, to give a satisfactory definition. The first of St. Thomas's arguments can be expressed in a single sentence: all things – the visible ones, the body, and also man's natural reason – all these things are good because they are created by God. "Omne ens est bonum" – this sentence occurring in the Western theory of being, which, incidentally, is quite Pauline, means simply: the world is good because it is creation; things are good insofar as they are creatures. The second argument comes from a sphere which is theological in a still more intensive sense; it derives from the theology of the sacraments: if visible things in their sacramental function become tools and vehicles of salvation, not only water, bread, and wine, but, above all, the human body – why then would all these not be good and worthy of affirmation, even demanding affirmation and reverence?

These arguments are in no way merely an "inner-theological" concern or just of purely theoretical interest. Instead, they are decisive for our practical attitude towards the world. In concrete terms, this theologically founded affirmation of natural reality means no less than that eros, technology, political power, science, the whole sphere of worldly things is declared as belonging – belonging, and, so to speak, having a right to vote in every aspect of Christian existence. Of course, this belonging also means something else. It includes the claim that the worldly sphere be formed and shaped according to the ultimate theological norms – in some way or other, but certainly in an existentially serious way.

As soon as one has this thought one sees very clearly what material for conflict is heaped up here, right at the heart of Western reality. But this is exactly the distinctive factor!

One recognizes this factor when a different reality comes into view, the non-Western. Recently, when some theologians of the Russian Orthodox Church visited West Germany, they expressed their surprise that there was such a thing here as the highly organized Church aid agencies – the Inner Mission and Caritas – using the most modern technology and following theological directives for the shaping of social life and the world of work. Such things have to be unimaginable for a religiosity which is completely taken up with the exercise of its ritual and with contemplation; they are unimaginable for a religiosity which is, on principle, unworldly, i.e., for a non-Western religiosity.

But Islam, too, is, despite its pugnaciously political aggressiveness, fundamentally unworldly. We did, in the twelfth and thirteenth centuries, come to know Aristotle through the mediation of the Arabs. But we alone have "received," in the genuine sense, this Greek knowledge of the world – knowledge which is open to being – and assimilated it into the interpretation of existence as handed down in Christian theology. Islam itself had no "reception" of Aristotle. The great Arab commentators of the medieval period were excluded from the religious community of Islam. What this separation of world and religion means in principle can be seen quite graphically from an event which is perhaps a well invented anecdote and yet, to my mind, has high value as a symptom. The prince of an Arabian house intends to have a telephone cable laid to his residence in the desert. In this, he has to overcome the grave doubts of his theologians, who explain that such a facility cannot be justified in the Koran. The prince got out of it by saying that he had Koran verses spoken through the telephone, and in this way he disarmed the theological resistance. It is important to see that with the kind of "biblical" otherworldliness of purely Koran religiosity it is fundamentally impossible to come to terms with or put a shape on worldly reality. Of course, what then happens with this worldly reality itself – inevitably – can be seen, in an historical experiment, from the "artificial" secularization and lack of roots manifested in the intellectual climate of modern Turkey.

But what is distinctively Western, as we have said, is the intrinsic link between existence in the world and religiosity: theologically grounded existence in the world, and theology that affirms the world and shapes it.

The combination of these two elements is explosive, because the link is endangered through nature. This means something further, namely, that the link cannot be achieved once and for all. With the model of a theologically grounded existence in the world a goal is formulated, but it cannot be expected that in some given moment a definitive balance can finally be achieved. Instead, it is a decision which has to be concretized and realized in every era. The West is not simply a fixed stock of institutions and achievements that could be passed on unchanged. The West is an historical *design* which, under constantly changing conditions, has to be converted, ever anew, into an historical reality.

This is why the correctives which counteract the

dissolution of the bond belong as part of the essence of the West – both the religious warnings against the "purely" worldly on the one hand and criticism of a narrow, one-sided religiosity on the other. These opposing voices, linked in counterpoint with one another, are also a specifically Western phenomenon. One could even say that being unsettled by the opposing component is what makes the West what it is.

Accordingly, two attitudes would be un-Western – and neither of them is a purely unreal construct. Instead, they constitute an extremely real danger which accompanies the whole of Western intellectual history. Un-Western would be both a religiosity undisturbed by any duty towards the world, and a worldly existence undisturbed by any call from beyond the world.

This gives us again, by way of negation, an answer to the question: what is the "Christian West"?

What Is, in Truth, Worth Preserving
A Speech about the rebuilding of the Paulinum Gymnasium in Münster (1959)

As soon as it became clear to me that what was expected of my contribution to this festive occasion was something that in old rhetorical parlance was called *Panegyrikós*; and that this could quite logically be expected of an old Pauliner (who, at Easter 1914, came into the sixth class, naturally not sensing what kind of a year that would be; and then after his Leaving year in 1923 was discharged into a world which, in the meantime, had undergone radical change; and then again some decades later, after a new World War, sent his sons to the same school – the youngest of them even for a couple of years to this very school, the same beautiful new building completed today) – when it became clear to me that I faced the task today of delivering a panegyric about the *schola Paulina*, immediately Plato's *Symposium* came to mind, which is nothing but a series of panegyrics (to Eros). More precisely, I was reminded of the comment made by , before it was his turn to speak, as he looked back on the speeches already made, particularly the last one. It had been a fascinating *poiema*, a work of art in words in which the musicality of the language achieved a truly magical effect. The audience was enchanted. Socrates himself also pretended, for a while, to be completely carried away – until, in a somewhat suspicious way, he fell into a tone of exaggeration: thinking of the speech he himself was about to make, he would have run away in shame if only he had known where to run; for he felt he was completely incapable of saying anything even approximating such beauty. "Above all, it occurred to me (as he said) what a laugh I have become for agreeing to join you in giving, each in turn, praise to Eros – since I obviously have no understanding of how one is to praise something. In my naivety I believed that one had to tell the truth about that which was to be praised . . . But that, as it seems, is not at all the case! Instead, what clearly matters is to say the most splendid and beautiful things possible, whether they are true or not. And if they happen to be false, that does not matter. – It seems we have not at all agreed to give real praise to Eros, but to pretend we are praising him – this pretence being meant for the ignorant, but of course not for the wise." Those are the words of Plato's *Symposium*.

There are two things truly worth noting in this ironic, completely Socratic comment. First, that here, in a way which stays fixed in the memory, a temptation is identified which can always confuse a person planning to give a panegyric – that he lose all sense of proportion, that he put aside the sober sense of reality and truth, and that he blindly and at random gather up praiseworthy elements, wherever he finds them, although they do not apply to the object of his praise; or that, with his hymn of praise, he inflates something of no substance, turning it into something wonderful. Under the uncompromisingly critical gaze of Plato's Socrates, a certain kind of declamation and pathos simply cannot flourish. It is just not possible to forget that nothing human is perfect and that in every human institution in this world, no matter how praiseworthy, there is a battle, and by no means always a victorious one, between what is right and superb, on the one hand, and wretched failure, narrowmindedness, laziness, guilt, and malice on the other. That does not mean that there is nothing at all to praise in the human sphere, and it does not make panegyrics impossible. But it does hinder one, also in this present case, from resorting to obvious possibilities for producing a very one-sided, facile eloquence, which exaggerates, and is unserious and detached. I am also asking myself what the expression on Socrates' face would be if the speaker wanted to make much of the plain fact of the many hundreds years of existence – of the fact that our *schola Paulina* is far more than a thousand years old and probably (as, when I was a pupil myself, I heard a speaker say, before the collapse of imperial Germany) "the oldest Gymnasium of the monarchy." I am not unaware how delicate and risky such heretical statements are when put to this gathering. However, I would like to tell you of a personal experience I had on the other side of the Atlantic, on the historically young soil of America. Not that I capitulated vis-à-vis the much scolded lack of respect for the past. Besides, I hardly experienced such lack of respect at any time "over there." Quite the contrary. Whenever, for example, I reported (well aware that this would make a considerable impression), not without pride, that I came from a school that had recently celebrated the 1150th year of its existence, it regularly caused not only enormous surprise but also a kind of reverential admiration. It was seen as an enviable thing, and people could hardly contain their feelings about it. The university newspaper which carried the usual interview with a visiting professor highlighted this fact the most in one separate headline: "His college more than eleven hundred years old" – or some such words. And now I found that, at bottom, I was unable to share this endearing and somewhat naive enthusiasm; that, almost to my own surprise, I could not quite identify with it. Suddenly I had "grasped" something, something obvious, also something that I had known in an "abstract" way for a long time: namely, that glory in human things is not to be found in the quantitative. For human beings the mere fact of the many hundreds of years of existence is basically of no relevance – unless it means at the same time passing the test of adherence to the good, by constant perseverance in what is right and true: this alone is something to boast about.

All this might seem to be extremely obvious. And it is. But the non-obvious begins as soon as one leaves the secure terrain of the quantitative – which is neutral. As soon as one decides to cut through the detachment of purely conventional compliments, toasts, and congratulations and ask straight out: what is – in content, *in concreto* – good and right, and, consequently, the sole aspect that is worthy of praise?

Here a second idea comes into play which Plato's Socrates, in his seemingly so innocent comment, suggests to us. It is the thought that praise and glorifying are unthinkable as a monolog of an isolated individual. On the contrary, the audience is part of it, a community with a somehow public character. Whoever wants to speak in praise needs, to be more precise, the acquiescence of an audience and agreement with it. One needs both – in regard to what is considered right and good and therefore meriting celebration and praise. As soon as this is said it becomes immediately clear what kind of oppressive current circumstances are involved. If we were not today here in Münster, but, let us say, in Leipzig or in Schulpforta, which was formerly so famous for its classical studies, this panegyric could not be held. In answer to the question what is there in the *schola Paulina* that is fundamentally right, good, and worthy of praise we can give the following answer: what is worth celebrating about this school is that, by virtue of its constitution, it makes room for things which, although of immeasurable worth for a truly human existence, are still not directly usable, not simply exploitable in the practical world of earning, utilization, production, fulfilling of (business) plans – and so on. It is worthy of praise that the *schola Paulina* is not purely focused on training (for perfect performance of a function) but above all on the education of the person, on the development of humanity in people; and that, while fully aware of the necessity to provide for material needs, it still affirms and respects the primacy of spiritual values; that it expressly does not promote what serves purely external goals, but also, and still more, what is meaningful in itself. Everyone knows that lauding such things in public speeches is impossible in totalitarian "workers" states, that it would be seen as hostile to the state. The partner – the audience – would be missing; the audience would remain silent because it would be forbidden to answer and to agree.

And yet, of course, it is not just a question of attitudes we associate with geographical regions – which we could characterize, for instance, with the term "the East". But the geographical does also deserve to be considered. In this we should not just be looking at the map of Germany, but at the globe – planet "earth". Recently in Berlin I had a conversation with the director of a humanistic Gymnasium, a school, incidentally which has very much in common with the Paulinum. We were standing, on a dark evening, in a garden a few hundred meters away from the border. My companion stretched out his hand and pointed to the east, saying: all that is dear to

our hearts is opposed by the state, starting from this border and extending to – Tokyo! Such terrifying perspec-
tives have one advantage: they destroy the illusion that
we could, by praising the advantages of a humanistic
education, run away from the world; as if we found ourselves in a separate space of triumphal unchallengeable
security. The considerations, the criticism, the negation
are also, as I have said, not geographically contained;
they have long since found their way into our own
thoughts. And it is doubtless healthy, and even necessary,
to expose ourselves to the force of the counter arguments
and to face them, just as our own arguments are always
in need of repeated scrutiny to see whether we can still
honestly make them our own.

For example, we can suspect from the start that not a
little of what nineteenth-century classicism introduced –
to the advantage of humanistic schools centered on
ancient classical languages – now meets with our indif-
ference. We know, in the meantime, too much about the
antiquity of Hellenism and Rome and also about the
great non-Western cultures, especially of the East, for us
to be able see in the so-called "classical antiquity" the
simply paradigmatic embodiment of the human as such
– to say nothing about the fact that, in our century, completely new dimensions of reality, until now unknown,
have emerged which now equally claim their place in our
necessarily limited field of vision.

Even the later Goethe, incidentally, who never
approached antiquity as a pure imitator, but, as
Nietzsche said of him "always as a competitor" (this is
what we read, for example, as something he said in conversation in his latter years: "People are always speaking
of the study of the ancients; but what does that mean

34

except: look at the real world and try to give expression to it, for that is what the ancients did too") – Goethe himself was already very much alive to the problematic implications of the (nineteenth-century) classicistic canonizing of the ancients. The old man does, indeed, show a visitor (from Westphalia, by the way) – a seemingly very gifted but unsettled young man with a wide variety of interests – "for his consolation," the mighty head of the ancient goddess "as a symbol that he persists with the Greeks and finds serenity there." But clearly Goethe himself is not altogether certain of the possibility of this "consolation." In any case, after the young man had gone, he said to Eckermann: "I am glad . . . I am not eighteen years old. When I was eighteen . . . it was still possible to do something; but now an incredible amount is demanded; . . . and in addition to that we are supposed to be Greeks and Romans!"

This last sentence sounds surprisingly familiar to us. It has been repeated in many different ways (not least by fathers with a humanist education who have taken the time to look over the shoulders of their adolescent sons as they study). Into this sigh of Goethe's in the year 1824 can be packed nearly everything that is said today against the humanistic school education in classical languages. This is approximately what it sounds like: how much must a young person today know and be able to do to take his place in modern society, which defines itself above all by technology, specialization and internationality. But that does not mean that it is a question of artificially and willfully forced demands; and we are not concerned with training for the highest leading functions, which, naturally, always require a special level of achievement. But let us think of the presuppositions for *any* kind of self-reliant collaboration in tasks aimed at achieving the common good – from satisfying hunger to providing military defense. How much here is not absolutely necessary! "And in addition to that we are supposed to be Greeks and Romans!" Why, then?

As we know, there is not a little that can be said in answer to this. We must admit, perhaps, that as reality opens up further and further it may become increasingly more difficult to be and to become an educated person – even if we leave aside the fact that, empirically, man has never been and will never be what it is "in him" to be. Whatever one means by "an educated person," what is at least required of him is that he possess more than the average knowledge of human nature. But precisely this knowledge (insofar as it can at all be gained by way of study) – one could say this in defense of studies of the classics – is to be had, more easily than anywhere else, through exposure to Greek and Roman antiquity. While it is certainly not a "model" (to be imitated), it does, however, serve as a practical instance, something like a structural model of non-transitory humanity. Furthermore, it could be said that the linguistic differentiation of Greek and the crystal-clear precision of Latin syntax offer the possibility of a formal schooling and discipline of the mind that is not to be found elsewhere, and which then – as has often been admitted – proves clearly advantageous to those involved in science and technology.

It is also difficult to refute the idea that leaders in intellectual life should have direct access to the great works of the ancient world – to Plato's dialogues, to the *Iliad* and the *Aeneid*, to the *Corpus Juris Civilis* – for these are simply the spiritual inheritance from which we are still living. Finally, there is the completely undeniable fact that in the area of world-European Western culture everyone, whether he knows it and likes it or not, in fact speaks Latin and Greek; that everyone who every day reads in the newspapers about atomic energy and radio activity, about rationalization and automation, about the Ecumenical Council, about programs and methods and specimens is constantly involved with the classical languages – and here the question should be added: whether a person could justifiably be called educated if he only half understands what he himself is saying.

However, it is not my intention to concern myself with a detailed discussion of individual arguments *"pro"* and *"contra"*; otherwise I would never be finished. There are many indications, by the way, that the decisive opinions originate from *outside* the sphere of rational argument – not independently of it, but, so to speak, one story lower. This by no means implies that one ought to, and justifiably can, dispense with thinking through the arguments and taking part in the debate. But if one were to forget that there are grounds which do not derive from and do not receive their cogency from *ratio* and which therefore cannot be shaken by it, one would – also in our case – be unjustifiably simplifying things.

Therefore I feel it is important to introduce another thought which (strangely!) has hardly ever been mentioned in this country – perhaps because it brings our attention to that deep dimension which underpins the rational and the cultural. In any case, it is an American whose idea is to be briefly reported here – an American who, so to speak, returned to Europe and then not only rediscovered the binding nature of the Western tradition with a quite new uninhibitedness but also expressed it in a carefree and frank manner which belongs to the best and most fortunate of things that that continent passes on to its sons. I am referring to *T.S. Eliot* – not so much the poet as the writer of philosophy, whose profound treatises on the concept of culture, the essence of the classical, the idea of a Christian society give him the authority to speak about the subject being treated here. He has done exactly that – and in an unusually energetic, almost aggressive way, in an essay on modern education and classical studies.

The aggressive aspect of T.S. Eliot's thought is aimed at sentimental Toryism which can yield up only a more or less flimsy justification for classical studies because it makes its justification depend on things which, at the most, have only relative importance. But it is high time to break through this dependence and to go back to a far superior, lasting foundation, from which alone the defense can derive its ultimate credibility. This foundation is the link of the classical languages with historical Christianity.

I do not think that this thesis of T.S. Eliot's – who himself had total command of ancient literature (one of his most important essays is about Virgil) – is saying that any one of the arguments already advanced is invalid. But: the "essential" validity and correctness of an argument is *one* thing; and it is a quite different thing whether the argument in fact impinges on the real thinking of the person – whether it is "existentially" effective. And this is what T.S. Eliot offers for consideration. The question to ponder: is it to be expected that in fact the "humanistic" justification for classical studies which is based on concepts like "education," "way of life," "culture" will be employed; and can one expect that this justification will stand up against the crude arguments of the practical sectors (economic, political, technological or military), which see their own claims as absolute? Is this to be expected *in the context of a fully secularized world*, a world in which there is no sacred book nor any sacred public ceremony, and for which, consequently, it can only be a curiosity that the languages of Church liturgy and of the New Testament are Latin and Greek – insofar as one is aware of this at all? Anyone who would see this as an unreal idea must, to my mind, know very little about the world in which we live.

To this question, which is his own, T.S. Eliot gives the following answer: "If Christianity is not to last any longer I won't be worried whether Latin and Greek texts fall into oblivion, just as the language of the Etruscans did, and become even more unintelligible than the latter." The sharp edge to this sentence did, I must confess, unsettle me when I first read it. And even today I can only suppose that the formulation is consciously exaggerated and deliberately one-sided. Still, there is this side to the issue, and I think it receives far too little attention. But as soon as it does receive this attention it may seem to us a little more plausible that one day schools of distinctly *Christian* character will be the ones to preserve and keep alive the inheritance of Greek and Roman antiquity – schools like the Pforta just mentioned, the restoration of which the German Evangelical Church seems to be considering, and the Gymnasium Paulinum, which has never denied its origins in the cathedral school of St. Ludger, and, to this day, still does not.

And here we find another – and not the least – of the things that cannot be passed over in a panegyric for the *schola Paulina*. Here I do not really mean, to be exact, the Christian aspect of this school. It is not fitting to praise someone just because he has received a gift; besides, there is the old saying: *optimorum non est laus* – originally, by the way, a Greek, Aristotelian sentence that means "what is best cannot be praised at all"; it cannot be reached by praise because it is removed from human judgment. Something different is to be praised here: namely, that the *schola Paulina* – and again by virtue of its constitution – has held firm to, preserved, kept alive, and handed down from one generation to another the gift, the inheritance entrusted to it, this quintessential *thesaurus*, this message which, as Plato has said, has come down to us from a divine source over the course of more than a thousand years; to put it differently, the school is, from its foundation to the present day, a place and a guarantor of *sacred tradition*.

Here a word has been mentioned which one can hardly avoid whenever there is talk of an institution that has existed for hundreds of years. The word "tradition," as everyone knows, has become loaded with many kinds of emotionally and ideologically influenced value judgments, both positive and negative. The result is that whoever undertakes, with this title in mind, to say anything celebratory, thereby enters a kind of arena. – But it cannot be difficult to reach agreement at least with regard to the following: tradition and the fostering of tradition are not things worth celebrating merely because what has "from time immemorial" been thought, said, and done simply continues to be thought, said, and done over the course of a hundred or a thousand years and even down to our own day. Rather: the glory of tradition –the content and the process of tradition – can only be seen as meaningful if, throughout the generations, *what is truly worth preserving* is preserved and continues to be preserved! – Of course, if things happen as they should, every young generation will continue to ask the critical question again: what is truly worth preserving? And the dialogue between the generations, which, most understandably, is and will be ever anew kindled by this question, should not be broken off by a rebellion of the young or be stopped by an authoritarian decree of the old. Certainly one will need to be prepared for the fact that one day the initial question in this dialogue will be formulated with a vehemence which up to now has not been known; to say it more concretely, the young will at some moment (and perhaps a not far-distant moment) cast doubt not on this or that custom but on "tradition" as such; that they will insist on asking how there can be any obligation to accept what has been thought, said, and done from time immemorial – why, and on what basis they should accept it? What rule is being infringed if what is handed down is simply left aside with a view to thinking, saying, and doing something fundamentally new!

One can only urgently hope that this radical question, which is comprehensive, is given a hearing and that an equally radical, comprehensive, serious answer may be heard – naturally, not "an" answer, not some answer or other, but the only true answer, the same as the one that is embodied in the real history of the *schola Paulina*; the answer, namely, that (and: why) there is – amongst the many things which are more or less worthy of preservation and which may be gathered under the heading of "tradition" – ultimately only *one* single traditional inheritance that it is absolutely necessary to preserve: the gift that is received and handed on in *sacred tradition*, received again, and handed on. I said that this answer is embodied in the history of the *schola Paulina*. But naturally it always needs to be articulated in the here and now; if it is to reach the questioner, the answer must be expressed convincingly – for example, by the fact that the answerer gives serious consideration to the reality of the present world; that he does not underestimate the weight of the counter arguments; and that, above all, he stands to his answer with his own existence.

This is now the right place for congratulations, congratulations on the entry to the new house – and, with this, my perhaps somewhat strange panegyric is to conclude. (It is, by the way, the same strangeness which keeps on occurring also in other circumstances and dismays us. On a particular occasion we innocently and lightheartedly set about celebrating the values of our Western inheritance – and then, under the gaze of the young generation, a gaze which is not particularly skeptical but simply questioning, though certainly looking for a convincing answer – then, unexpectedly, it becomes clear that we ourselves are being challenged to make a decision we have not yet made: where we stand, seriously and without rhetoric – given the fundamental changes the world has undergone – with regard to the current seemingly unchallengeable values.) And if now my congratulations, which I give with deep joy and attachment, take up the old formula: "*schola Paulina vivat, crescat, floreat,*" then this is what I mean: may it be granted to the pupils and teachers, the young and the old Pauliners, to preserve in truth what is worth preserving, to receive it and to hand it on; and may you increase the glory of your four-hundred-year-old school by unwaveringly affirming and realizing all that is praiseworthy in it!

Death and Immortality

Whoever ponders the question: what really happens when a person dies? – such a one is asking about much more than a particular point where, on a given date, something occurs. And it is precisely this much wider ranging question which becomes insistent and unavoidable as soon as, with complete openness, we face up to the deep distress which confrontation with death brings with it. When faced with the death of persons who are close to us we cannot escape asking questions about God and the world; more precisely, it is a question about man, about ourselves – not so much what man is (a definition is not urgently needed, nor is a description of the nature of man – such discussion will seem only too insipid, almost unserious, to the person who has been affected by the presence of death) – no, what is urgently needed is an answer to the question about human existence and its ultimate meaning.

Augustine speaks, in the fourth book of his *Confessions*, of the death of a friend which struck at his very existence when he was nineteen years old. "My soul could not live without him." But they had parted at the end almost in conflict with one another: his friend, as he lay there unconscious and in a fever, had been baptized; and then it seemed as if he would survive the sickness; Augustine visits him and, as he himself reports, "expecting applause, jokes about the baptism which he had received completely without knowledge and awareness". But his sick friend, with unexpected severity, calls Augustine – now completely taken aback and stunned – to order. Augustine, full of embarrassment, goes on speaking: well, he should get his strength back (and so forth) – and he concludes his visit. But the fever returns and the friend dies before Augustine returns. "Then it became dark in my heart, and wherever I looked I only saw death . . . I hated everything . . . I had become a big question to myself"; *factus eram ipse mihi magna quaestio.* It has very rightly been said: here is "the birth of existential philosophy" from the experience of man's fate in confrontation with death.

And so death is a philosophical theme of a quite particular kind. There are quite important voices, from antiquity down to the present, that say: Philosophizing, i.e. the pondering on the whole of existence, is nothing but a meditation on death, *commentatio mortis* (this is found in Cicero in his *Tusculan Disputations*), and: death is the genius that inspires philosophy, and without it philosophy is hardly possible (Schopenhauer says).

Another word needs to be said about the formulation "death and immortality." Both of these concepts linked in the theme of this investigation will, on average, be taken by the naive reader or listener to mean that "death" is, so to speak, the question and "immortality" the answer – the answer, above all, of the Christian philosopher; that the tormenting problem of "death" is solved and resolved in the certainty of "immortality. his supposition and the expectations connected with it must be clearly and energetically contradicted from the start. This is not what is meant. It is not *possible* for it to mean this – not if the Christian message or the message of Plato's Socrates is taken seriously. This is not to say that the "immortality of the soul" is unreal or not to be proven – of course not. The level of mind, even of the human mind, shows in its indestructibility. But this does not tell us what is meant by the conquering of death. This happens not simply by the soul, as if not at all affected (by death), continuing to exist beyond the disintegration of the body. Here I must quote Augustine again – from his monologues: "When you have found out (he asks as he ponders) that you are immortal: is that enough for you?" The answer is: "It is surely a great thing, but for me it is too little."

The continued existence of the soul as if it were not affected by death – this casually used formulation leads us to the kernel of the problem. If, namely, what happens to a person in dying can meaningfully and logically be called "separation of body and soul" (this formulation, which has been embedded in human language for some thousands of years, can have a claim to classical status although it is mainly an attempted description – which does not explain anything) - , if, then, we accept this descriptive characterization, then the interpretation of death (more precisely: of dying) depends on how that which is separated in the process of dying is thought to be connected in the first place – in life. Are body and soul to be thought of as combined in such a way that no real *unity* of being comes about, that, fundamentally, they are always two things (for example, the soul is something like a tradesman using his body like a piece of technical equipment; or: the soul, like a boatman who, when he lands (in dying!), leaves the boat like something he no longer needs); or if body and soul are thought of as two beings forcibly locked together, almost against their nature, one hindering and disturbing the other, the body the prison of the soul – it is completely clear that then the separation of body and soul – dying – must mean something fundamentally other than when the combination of body and soul is conceived of as *one* single being – just as when out of a small piece of silver and the shape impressed on it (an image, a coat of arms, an eagle) a coin is made. And that idea is the model used to conceive of the relationship between body and soul from antiquity down to our own day: *anima forma corporis*, the soul is the form which molds the body from within, giving it its shape. Whoever sees the combination of body and soul such that both together constitute the one living person (not that the soul is the "real" person who uses the body (*homo est anima utens corpore*, as Thomas Aquinas characterizes Plato's conception); but, rather: body and soul belong together by nature, on the basis of the nature of *both*; both friends with one another, both dependent on one another, not just the body on the soul, but also the soul relying on the body for development of life) – and this view has been confirmed a thousandfold by empirical research on real human life and is confirmed ever anew, and indeed in both directions, not only in the direction of a "materialistic" interpretation of human nature: that, namely, that there is nothing "purely" spiritual in man, nothing, for example, that is only thought, only spiritual act and not simultaneously sense life and organic function; no, confirmation by empirical anthropology of the old teaching about the *anima forma corporis* points equally in the other direction: that in man there is nothing "purely" material, "purely" bodily, "purely" biological, but that, instead, organic life, in all its dimensions, including the vegetative, is influenced, "formed" by the attitude and decisions of the spiritual soul – again: if we understand the link between body and soul like this, as the combination by virtue of which we live in the body, we must look on death, the separation of body and soul, as an event that leaves no aspect of our existence, no element of our nature untouched and uninvolved.

Here can be seen the lack of precision, the inappropriateness of the language customarily used to speak about the "immortality of the soul." Strictly speaking, looking at it from a linguistic point of view, it is not for the body, and it is not for the soul to die, to be mortal or even immortal – just as we also know that it is not real, but figurative language, to say of granite or of fame that they are immortal, or to speak of undying disgrace: granite, fame, disgrace are not of the kind that permits us to predicate of them, in the strict sense, dying or not dying. But the soul is not like that, nor is the human body. If we take the exact meaning of the words, it is not the soul that is immortal, nor is it the body that dies. The person dies, the whole person made up of body and soul. And if, in regard to man, there can be talk of immortality in the strict sense of the word, then this immortality has to be attributed not to the soul but to the whole man. And this is exactly the way the New Testament, as well as classical theology, speaks about immortality; the concept "immortal soul" is as good as unknown there, whereas by contrast it is said of the risen Christ, of man in paradise, of man in the future eon – and, indeed, only of them – that they are immortal.

Another matter that concerns discussion of the "immortal soul" is the fact that the origin of this term is somewhat revealing and arouses suspicion: it is a question of the formula for "the really central dogma of the Enlightenment"; it comes from the same type of calming philosophy against which the materialist Ludwig Feuerbach rightly introduced the concept of an "apparent death" because it attempts to falsify man's earthly end to make of it a process which does not affect the soul. This is, namely, what the Enlightenment's notion of immortality mainly says: first, that death is more or less something unreal; a mere transition; something that fundamentally does not concern the spiritual person; and second: life after death is the continued life of the "soul," a continued existence in the strictest sense and therefore a better life insofar as the soul (I quote the old Enlightenment philosopher Reimarus) "is raised from a more imperfect life of the senses to a more perfect, everlasting life of the spirit" which is now no longer constricted by the body.

The fact that, in hearing this, we are reminded of Plato is part of the success of that Enlightenment philosophy and its misinterpretation of Plato – if not to say its falsification of Plato. That is a severe expression, but I fear that Moses Mendelssohn's "Phaedo or on Immortality" can hardly be described otherwise. This book, written in 1767, was one of the most successful books of German Enlightenment philosophy. It is also a strange book. There are long passages which are simply a translation of Plato's *Phaedo*. But the reader has no way of knowing what is literal translation and what is Mendelssohn's own text. Mendelssohn does explicitly say in his preface that he has "tried to adjust the metaphysical proofs to suit the taste of our times"; but these deviations have in no way been made recognizable; and if we compare Mendelssohn's *Phaedo* with that of Plato we find that precisely the crucial part of Plato's text has been omitted. For example, it is not possible to see that Plato expressly avoids all rational speculation about the life of the soul after death and that, instead, he only calls on the myth, amongst the fundamental characteristics of which is that Plato is not its author; but, above all, the unsuspecting reader of Mendelssohn's *Phaedo* has no chance of finding out that, in Plato's opinion, the naked continuation of existence of the soul is by no means desirable in itself; that, on the contrary, as Socrates says, for the person who does not want the good, immortality is a frightening prospect, and that it is therefore a quite different thing – something that goes beyond a mere further existence – which makes life of the soul after death something man would hope for. What Mendelssohn completely leaves out is Plato's explicit teaching that this world and the "other" are separated not just by death, in which body and soul are separated, but by (the last) judgment – and so on. Naturally this is not the place to go into detail. But what is important is that this misinterpretation of Plato still has an influence through widespread popular philosophy, and through literature, right down to our own day – so that the Enlightenment conception of immortality is unquestioningly identified with that of Plato, with the result that Plato – in this point completely inaccurately – is seen to be incompatible with the Christian view of death, the indestructibility of the soul, and life after death.

But let me go back: if you understand concrete man as by nature a bodily being (and "by nature" always means for the Christian "by virtue of creation") it is impossible to think of and interpret the indestructibility of the soul as if this part of ourself simply "lives on" and "continues to exist" simply, i.e. as if death had not at all touched and affected the soul. Such a misleading "coping with death" is no longer possible for us, it seems to me, if we really take seriously what empirical research about the human being has brought to light. We are just not able to manage it any more. We cannot do it. Even the materialistic interpretation would seem more plausible to us. Of course, this too is an inadmissible simplification. Here two things have to be thought together (and therein lies the difficulty from time immemorial): on the one hand, that the whole person, body and soul, is touched and affected by death, and yet, on the other hand, that the soul remains in being and is not destroyed.

The effect on the whole person brought about by death is called "end": if the togetherness of body and soul constitutes the existence of the living person, then death is *eo ipso* the end of this unity. With the separation of body and soul there is not a separation of two things (the boatman leaves the boat); but: the *one* being "man," who not only "lives" but also has continued existence through the union of body and soul, ceases to be. A dead person *is* really not a person at all! Here, language comes to the limit of its ability to name things. We can say: the dead (person) – but who is that supposed to be? The body deprived of its soul, the corpse? "How should we bury 'you'" – this is the question the pragmatist Crito (in Plato's *Phaedo* dialogue) puts to the condemned Socrates in the last hour before the end. Socrates' answer is well known: "Do what you think fit – should you manage to take hold of 'me' and 'I' do not escape you" – an answer which in one point is completely appropriate: what is being buried is not Socrates! A much more radical formulation is to be found in Aquinas's commentary on Aristotle: strictly speaking, what ceases to remain after death is not only the bodily living thing, but, in a completely different meaning of the word, it can be said of the members of the body. Flesh and blood – perhaps that can be said to remain. But it is not really possible to talk

of the "hand" after death. Only a living hand, one
informed by the soul, is, to be precise, a hand! That is a
hard, almost brutal thing to say, but it only formulates
the unavoidable consequence of man's existing through
the union of body and soul and not being "man" in the
full sense after death – whatever remains in being.

However, when a person dies, something else happens at the same time which is an "end" in a much deeper sense than this natural process of the separation of
body and soul. This leave-taking of body and soul has to
be described as a natural occurrence. Even in a death that
is willingly accepted or caused – for example, the death
of a martyr or an act of suicide – the separation of body
and soul is not directly brought about by the person concerned: we are not the ones who bring about the separation; on the contrary, even when we take our own lives,
death happens to us. It comes over us as an objective
event from outside. But along with this objective process
something subjective also happens in death; and this
subjective element also means an "end" – and, indeed, an
end of such a kind that the finality of the separation of
body and soul seems to be surpassed by far. We can also
put it this way: in death it is not just the end that comes
about; but the person, as person, i.e. as a being that is not
only both capable of making a decision and called to it
but also is unable to avoid it – this person "makes" an
end. Not that it is in his power to die or not to die; he
must die, and the separation of body and soul which he
cannot bring about or prevent comes over him like a natural event. And as a "creature" he resists this overpowering, with all the fear of the creature and with all the wild
drive of the natural will to live. But in the middle of it or
perhaps even in the very last moment of this resistance

(when the hopelessness of his struggle has finally become evident), the person is confronted with the challenge – even the necessity – to make a decision, i.e. to perform a free act. When dying he is in a situation where he can do nothing but "achieve" his own death in a free decision, and to take on, of himself, total responsibility for himself. For the first and only time in his life he is required to do this – but also enabled to do it – so that it has rightly been said: the supreme act of life on earth is precisely the one that ends it.

It is necessary to see here that necessity and freedom are linked. To leave out one of the two elements – the necessitating element from outside us or the element of free decision – is to get it wrong. In Heidegger's idea of death as "my own possibility" or as "freedom to die," the element of necessity, of passive helplessness, is obscured. For this reason I think Sartre was right in his objection (to Heidegger): that death is a fact, simply an objective event "that, of its nature, happens independently of me," *un pur fait, comme la naissance* (a pure fact, like birth). Death is not "my possibility" any more than birth is. Sartre, I think, is right in his objection to Heidegger; but overall he too has got it wrong: death is not a "mere" fact that happens to us and overpowers us.

The aspect of freedom and decision in death (more precisely: dying) becomes clearer from the idea of ending the *status viatoris* handed down to us. I do not want to employ the traditional terms "pilgrimage" or "state of pilgrimage." The insight contained in the (Latin) term should not be distorted and spoilt through the influence of misleading connotations. The term has nothing to do with feeling or sentimentality. It does not even have a specifically religious meaning or anything like an ethical demand (to make progress, to become better, etc. – however natural such requirements are). What is meant by the *status viatoris* and the conclusion of it is: as long as a person exists bodily, he finds himself, whether he likes it or not, on a journey; he can stand still, make detours, go back (in a certain sense), go astray; he can also go ahead in the right direction – he has countless possibilities. Only one possibility is not open to him: the possibility of not being on a journey, not being on the way, *in via*. But there is a moment when this state of being on the way is ended, which means that from this moment on there is no longer the possibility of making further progress, of standing still, of going astray, making detours! From this moment on the person is no longer "on the way"; and that is the moment of death. Dying means ending the journey as well as the inner state of being on the way. This ending is therefore an act which takes place in the core of the person, the innermost region where the decision is formed.

No matter how suddenly and unexpectedly death comes as an external event that catches us unawares: the decision required of me by necessity, possibly from one moment to another, this free decision concerning the whole of my life, constitutes the last step on the way. Despite all appearances there are many indications that this final decision is not hindered by any kind of time pressure. We know that in a split second we can dream an occurrence that stretches over a number of years and that to carry out a spiritual act (for example, of loving attention) requires a minimal amount of time; it is also known, for instance, that people who were saved from the immediate threat of death saw, in the last moment before the loss of consciousness, the whole of their lives unfolded before their eyes with full clarity and with all the details they had long since forgotten – which we could be justified in seeing as challenging, or at least as enabling, a full evaluation of this same life, now by the highest definitive standard. Precisely this would be the final step on the way, the step by which man achieves his "ultimate state." The act in which this happens could well be considered a completely unarticulated sigh, heard by no one, the sigh of *conversio ad Deum* which is perhaps hidden from one's own reflex consciousness, the turning to the ultimate foundation of being (of course, there is the possibility of a turning away, the *aversio*).

The meaning of death as the ending of the *status viatoris* is that every human life is going to an end and coming to an end, and does not simply stop at some moment. There is no death – no matter how much it "happens" from outside and as a natural occurrence – that is simply a breaking off of vital functions. Dying is also always at the same time an act that expressly concludes existence from within, an execution, a sealing, a bringing to an end, a signature and completion of the totality of one's life, a finalizing, a completion, a decision. What is meant, above all, is that, strictly speaking, there is in no such thing as an untimely or premature death.

When Sartre maintains that death cannot have the character of a "final chord" if only for the reason that chance determines the moment it occurs ("We should be compared with a man condemned to death, who is bravely preparing himself for the last walk, concentrating on cutting a good figure on the gallows, and in the meantime is taken off by an influenza epidemic") – his formulation is witty and, moreover, by comparison with a desperate Stoic attitude of being "prepared for death," completely to the point. But he does not express the true meaning. And when Sartre speaks of the young author with promise of being a great writer who then dies "prematurely," the reply must be: Sartre seems not to have seen the journey, the ending of which is under discussion here; he seems not to see the inner point of expectation to which human self-realization is orientated and for which it is designed.

In discussion about the death penalty it is occasionally said that execution takes man's own death away from him. I do not just see this as being no argument against the death penalty. It is also intrinsically irrelevant. If there could be such a thing as being "robbed of one's own death" one would need to think of what I read about in America: the deceiving, by use of every means – from suggestion to the use of drugs – of terminally ill patients who purposely pay for it in certain cosmopolitan cities. It has been said that in comparison with these (who, of course, despite everything, can hardly be dispensed from making their own final decision or be robbed of it) the man condemned to death is in a happy position.

In other words: it is one of the indestructible certainties of human existence that death, beyond the purely natural event that separates body and soul, is, in an incomparably more intense way, the "end": the ending of an inner journey, brought about in a definitive free decision that concerns one's whole existence.

But this idea of the ending of the *status viatoris* contains also a quite different element: the orientation towards the future. The definitive act that finishes and brings about the end does not only – and not primarily – have the past in mind. This is true even for the external order – in relation to sons and heirs. But orientation towards the future is even more significant in the act which establishes inner order concerning one's existence as a whole. Dying does mean "ending of a journey," "completing the course." But it is naturally contrary to the obvious sense of such ideas that now the "journeying" and "doing the course" is essentially over. The hope incorporated in the very existence of the *viator* is not directed at the mere cessation of the pilgrimage but at *arrival* at the destination. Although, therefore, the concept of ending the *status viatoris* has the extremely intense meaning of end and finality, it also includes the element of "transition" and therefore "not ending." When we think of death as the ending of the inner journey we, at the same time, include the notion of the indestructibility of the soul.

But what does this indestructibility of the soul mean? In a nutshell: it is not only impossible for the human soul simply to disappear from reality – either by destruction coming from outside or through a decision taken, an opting for nothingness; but the human soul is, not of its own doing, but by virtue of the nature given it in creation, endowed with such stability and invulnerability that, beyond death and physical decay, it continues in being as itself and with its identical individuality.

If one asks about the arguments which could support or prove this thesis, the first consideration must be, what kind of "argument" could be expected. Clearly, we are not in the realm of direct experience, and so it is immediately obvious that a purely empirical "proof" is not possible. Still less are we in the realm of the quantitative, which means that nothing can be achieved through measurement and computation. The biologist Adolf Portmann has said that "no one will derive from present-day research in the natural sciences a scientific explanation of the origin and purpose of living things and that this is no less true of flowers and birds than it is of us human beings"; this is as much as to say that "the biologist has no competence to answer the question about immortality." The following sentence from Sigmund Freud seems to me to have more the character of an argument, although Freud himself did not attribute to it any value as evidence (yet he did insist that it was an empirically founded statement): "In the unconscious, every one of us is convinced of his immortality." One can logically doubt, it seems to me, that all men, in the unconscious zone of their spiritual life, can be totally deceived about such a fundamental aspect of their existence. But this is still not an argument in the strict sense – *if* by argument we mean one which is acquired through the scientific penetration of the reality under discussion, namely, the soul itself. – The question is whether there are such arguments for the indestructibility of the soul. Certainly, for a few thousand years, proofs have been formulated which make precisely this claim. If one tries to put some order into them, they reduce to a dozen different basic categories. All of these arguments, if their claim is not immediately to be dismissed, have to stand up to the experience that at first sight seems irrefutable, that in death all signs of life – even the spiritual ones – cease. They have to make clear, from what one encounters in the reality of the soul, that the soul cannot be swept along and included in the destruction and dissolution of the body. This is precisely the claim of all those arguments, whether they are based on the soul's "simplicity," "immateriality," "spirituality," or "transcendence of time," or whatever else.

It seems clear that people have different affinities to a given particular argument, so that the other arguments have little appeal to them. The argument that says the most to me is that of the soul's capacity for truth. This is to be found both in Plato and in Augustine and Thomas. In the *Summa theologica* we read: Because the soul is *capax veritatis* (capable of truth) it is therefore also immortal. This latter clause is a conclusion. Its validity can only be understood, of course, by someone who has understood the content of the preceding clause. When dealing with the quantitative, looking at the hand on the dial yields the required result; but here I have to know what truth is and what constitutes knowledge of truth; I must "see" that knowing the truth, despite all our radical dependence on our physical organs, is a process which is fundamentally independent of all physiological processes. To be aware of precisely this in the phenomenon itself – and also to recognize it – is the essential and difficult factor. Still, this argument is in fact admitted by everyone – even by those who deny it, for everyone who uses human utterance, i.e. everyone who wants to make (an aspect of) reality known and communicate something is essentially laying claim to a validity which could never be the result of material processes. In the same moment as one can show that an utterance is the result of material processes one has already shown that it does not possess the validity of really human speech. And naturally there *are* such utterances which neither make (an aspect of) reality known nor communicate anything. The brain surgeon knows that the stimulation of certain centers, for instance in an operation, triggers off the language motor; but no one would take such utterances to be "human speech." There is also a purely associative thinking and speaking that follows a chance idea and is also likewise to a large extent the result of psychic and physiological mechanisms. Above all, there is "ideological" thinking that amounts to nothing more than a reflex of more or less material interests; in the very moment when this is seen, such thinking and speaking loses its value. The generally legitimate influence of Marxism is based precisely on the fact that a methodical principle can show that certain political opinions – and some based on weltanschauung – are in fact worthless *because* they are the result of material conditions. But this very fact supports, on the other hand, the notion that a claim to truth is only valid on the basis of its independence of all non-spiritual causality. Even if someone maintains that *all* human opinions come about, without exception, by virtue of mechanical necessity – for instance, as a result of conditions of production and class – he is necessarily and as a matter of course making an exception of his own thesis. To have any claim to validity, it has to have come about in a different way: as an objective grasp of reality, i.e. as knowledge of *truth*. This again proves that no one takes a human idea seriously that has come about through a non-spiritual causality, i.e. an idea which is not independent of all material processes.

The argument for the indestructibility of the soul, the argument from the possibility of truth, is as follows: because the human soul is *capax veritatis*, because it is able to grasp truth, because it is able to do something that is, in principle, beyond and independent of every conceivable material process, it must also have an *esse absolutum*, i.e. *being* that is independent of matter, independent of the body; it must necessarily be something that survives as real during the disintegration of the body and beyond.

Of course, what kind of survival this is, how the being of the soul, the *anima separata*, will be constituted after death – of these things we have no reliable human knowledge. And we can almost identify the great minds by the fact that they explicitly lay no claim to such knowledge. We know them by their silence. In Plato, as I have said, we find no rational speculation about what happens to man after death. Even the sacred books of Christendom have little more to say than to speak of "being asleep." But this word should be considered more precisely than is usually the case. Those who are asleep and those who are in a state of ecstasy enter a sphere of existence in which, for example, they abide in a new non-temporal mode in which our clocks and measures of time are irrelevant; those who are in ecstasy, dreaming, sleeping are receptive in a higher way, more receptive to the influence of forces which, while unknown, reach the innermost self. In Novalis's *Fragments* we read that a "person who has died" is one who has been "raised into an absolute, mysterious state." Precisely our normal idea of time has, as we have said, lost its validity; the "time in between," which stretches from the moment of our death to the resurrection we hope for, in faith, at the end of time, cannot be of the same kind as between birth and death. But that is more a negative than a positive statement. Anything more is beyond the range of our cognitive powers.

However, even information of this negative kind is of no small value. It provides room for dealing with other quite positive assumptions, which of course can only be available to the believer. Anyone, for example, who has the vivid experience that human life consists in the mutual interaction between body and soul and understands death as the end of the real bodily and spiritual person, will not be able to answer the question: how a "departed" soul which is separated from the body is to be conceived of as "existing" at all, not to say as being "alive." This puzzle, which cannot be solved by pure theoretical speculation, could, it seems to me, in a completely new way, make the truth of faith about the resurrection audible – not comprehensible, but audible, perhaps also only more audible.

At this point of the discussion I will break off – on the threshold which separates the sphere of philosophy from that of theology and which I have perhaps already slightly crossed. It only remains for me to quote a word from Kierkegaard's "Closing unscientific postscript to the philosophical crumbs": "Glory be to erudition, and glory to the one who can bring his erudition to bear on the erudite question about immortality. But the question about immortality is essentially not an erudite question. It is a question about the inner life that the subject, acting subjectively, must ask himself."

Immortality – a Non-Christian Idea?
Philosophical comments on a controversial theological theme

1

The reason for the following comments is a thesis contained in a treatise by Oscar Cullmann on "The immortality of the Soul and the Resurrection from the Dead. The Witness of the New Testament." An interpretation of this thesis that goes further than Cullmann's view is contained in a lengthy review in the international periodical *Novum Testamentum*, which appears in Leiden. Cullmann says: "If we ask an average Christian, whether Protestant or Catholic, intellectual or not, what the New Testament teaches about the individual fate of man after death, we will, with few exceptions, receive the answer: 'the immortality of the soul.' Expressed like this, however, this view is one of the greatest misunderstandings of Christianity." In our present context only the last sentence in this quotation is of interest: it is a misunderstanding that the New Testament teaches the immortality of the soul. The sentence allows of several interpretations. But what is clearly meant is that the idea of immortality of the soul has nothing to do with, or is even incompatible with the teaching of the New Testament about what happens to a person after death. Cullmann speaks explicitly about "incompatibility": "The teaching of the great Socrates and of the greater Plato *cannot be reconciled* with the teaching of the New Testament." This is also how the reviewer of the periodical *Novum Testamentum* understood Cullmann's thesis. Until now, he writes, he had remained of the opinion, especially following the argument of Gerardus van der Leeuw, "that the New Testament knew both immortality *and* resurrection. Cullmann's study has led me to the conviction that the New Testament in fact only deals with the resurrection." "Immortality is an idea of Greek philosophy, and this idea has nothing to do with resurrection in the Bible."

2

The reference to Gerardus van der Leeuw indicates that the idea is not entirely new. In fact, we find in van der Leeuw's *Phenomenology of Religion*, in 1933, the sentence: "The Christian faith knows not immortality but resurrection, i.e. new creation." Paul Althaus had, a long time ago, already spoken, in his eschatology, of the sharp contrast between "the notion of the continued life of the soul" and the central New Testament idea of the resurrection. And Luther himself, as it seems, treated with irony the decree of the Fifth Lateran Council (1512–1517) according to which it was "a plague" to consider the spiritual soul of man to be mortal. Carl Stange, in his monograph about the immortality of the soul, makes the comment: Luther "was clear in his mind that the teaching of the Catholic church at this point was under the influence of Greek philosophy and contrary to the Christian view." Similar formulations are often found in Evangelical theology; but Oscar Cullmann's view is far more extreme than anything said above. The periodical *Novum Testamentum* sums up Cullmann's treatise in one sentence: "Therefore, in the New Testament it is taught that not only the body but also the soul dies." The most surprising aspect of this sentence is, it seems to me, its complete agreement with what is said in the Marxist weltanschauung.

3

If we try to understand and to formulate what is behind this thesis and is being proclaimed in it, we discover, above all, the endeavour to keep before our minds the completely "supernatural" reality of the resurrection and of eternal life as something which is, beyond all question, absolute – something which depends on grace and which cannot be achieved through any purely human, "natural" power. But this absolute character, with its dependence on grace, seems to be relativized by the thought of an immortality which the soul has by its very nature ("so that therefore the resurrection of the body almost appears to be little more than an 'accessory' that could almost as easily be left out"). Above all, if the supposition is that the soul lives on by virtue of its own nature, death seems to forfeit its reality. But if death is nothing genuinely real that affects the whole person, how am I to believe that the overcoming of death through the resurrection and eternal life are *the* decisive fruit of the salvation that comes to us in grace through Christ? "Resurrection: that is the grave *forced open* . . . Immortality: that is the grave denied" – as Helmuth Thielicke formulates it with epigrammatic precision. Moreover, also in this point there is a natural affinity to *materialism*: It is Ludwig Feuerbach who, to counter the "the shallow immortality doctrine" of enlightenment theology, formulated the polemical – but nonetheless serious – concept of "apparent death": if the soul, in death, only undergoes something like a "change of location" and simply "lives on," is death not then mere appearance? Feuerbach counters with the thesis: in death, the person simply ceases to be, both in body and soul. (Exactly this, we are told today, is the teaching of the New Testament: ". . . the soul dies also.")

4

The outline offered here and the attempt to interpret the thesis with regard to the issues involved in it, is, it seems to me, polemical *in three ways*: *first*, against the idea of immortality as found in the philosophy and theology of the enlightenment; *second*, against the "Greek" – or more precisely, the Platonic – doctrine of immortality; *third*, against Catholic theology, *insofar* as it accepts the "purely philosophical," "heathen" element of the Greek argument for immortality and tries to link it with the teaching of the New Testament.

It is clear that with the two last-named points the challenging character is to some extent delineated which is contained in that thesis and constitutes the reason for the following discussion. To put it concretely (and a little primitively), the Catholic Christian fundamentally believes that the "heathen," "Greek," "philosophical" origin of an idea is *not eo ipso* an argument against its truth; but, if not against its truth, then also not against its belonging to Christian truth or even against its compatibility with Christian truth. – There is naturally a further challenge for the philosopher who is engaged in the – in many ways – problematic business of philosophical reflection on reality: only on the basis of weighty arguments will he accept the view that the teaching of Plato – one of the ancestors of all Western philosophizing – on the nature of man and on the structure of his existence is simply not accurate or is irrelevant; he will even incline to the opinion that it takes no little effort, even to gain an accurate *grasp*, for example, of the very differentiated Platonic teaching of the life of the soul after death.

I believe that there is, in fact, a considerable measure of misunderstanding, misinterpretation, and non-admissible simplification involved here. Above all, it can be shown to be false to identify the enlightenment notion of immortality with that of Plato. They simply have nothing to do with one another. This is even more true of the immortality argument of the great scholastics (in Stange's monograph we read: "There is really no great distinction between the idea of immortality of the enlightenment and that of the medieval period.").

5

It does not require many words to show that the doctrine of immortality as formulated by Rousseau and, after him, in some of the influential writings of the late 18th and early 19th centuries by Moses Mendelssohn, Lessing and Reimarus (or in Christoph August Tiedge's successful book "Urania" which appeared in 1801 and was declaimed in all the salons at the time and elicited some very biting comments from Goethe; the final verses of the last canto, entitled "Immortality," read: "A *man*, a tired pilgrim finishes his journey / A *god* sets out on his") – it is easy to show that *this* view of immortality, which is, moreover, *the* really central dogma of the Enlightenment, is simply incompatible with the New Testament. The quintessence of this teaching is that after death, which does not really affect the spiritual aspect of the person, the soul continues to exist in a "better" life – on the strength of its own moral power; this "other" life is "better" because the constraints and conditions of *earthly* life are overcome (only insofar as he belongs to the world of senses is man, in this view, "a needy being" – words of Immanuel Kant, by the way). It can be said, therefore, that in the thinking of the Enlightenment this notion of a purely spiritual continued existence, free of need and earned by the fulfillment of one's duties, takes over the place which, in the faith of a Christian, is occupied by "eternal life." And it is even explicitly said that the New Testament itself teaches this: according to Lessing in his *Education of the Human Race*, Christ is "the first reliable, practical teacher of the immortality of the soul." Nothing is clearer than that Christian theology had to distance itself energetically from such a claim. If it is certainly true (something which I am not in a position to judge, but which is stated in the handbook *Religion in Geschichte und Gegenwart*) that this is the historical foundation for the fact that the concept of immortality, in the most recent Evangelical theology, was excluded from dogmatic discussion as something which did not belong, then I must confess that I find this incomprehensible. As I have said, that degenerate "enlightened" doctrine of immortality has nothing to do with the classical philosophical theory of immortality that we find formulated in Plato or also in Thomas Aquinas.

6

Of course, with regard to Plato's theory the situation involves great complexity. One of the books on the theme of "immortality" that stem from the German Enlightenment period and even today have a widespread influence through popular philosophy and literature is that of Moses Mendelssohn, Lessing's friend. His "Phaedo" presents itself as an interpretation of Plato, almost a work of Plato himself, while textual comparison shows that Mendelssohn's "Phaedo," in which, without any open statement, Plato's text and Mendelssohn's own statements are merged, really amounts to a falsification of Plato's teaching – not just in minor matters but in the basic conception. A further, almost insuperable complication results from the fact that also the scholarly historical Plato interpretations (from Hegel and Zeller down to Wilamowitz), on the basis of the same rationalistic stance, seem to confirm and give weight to the falsification, while on the other hand "for contemporaries (= Mendelssohn's), . . . who had given up revelation and yet wanted to resist the rising tide of materialism, . . . this book (= "Phaedo") was not a mere philosophical teaching but, in truth, a book of religious edification and consolation." (That here again the materialist position is named as part of an obviously unavoidable alternative seems to me not lacking in significance.)

7

This is where the formal treatment of the topic should begin. Naturally, the theme is inexhaustible. In accordance with the double challenge already indicated, which for me is contained in the denial of the idea of immortality, I would like, in what follows, to limit myself to the discussion of two points: to a thesis-like exposition of the *Platonic* doctrine of the continued life of the human soul after death. I will not be concerned so much with expounding the arguments used in the Platonic dialogues to prove the indestructibility of the soul as to showing what, in Plato's view, life after death will be like. And I will stress precisely those aspects which highlight the difference or the contrast between what Plato really says and what on the basis of an "enlightened" secularist misinterpretation is, down to our own day, broadly accepted as being Plato's own opinion. – Second, I would like to try – again in brief summary – to explain how, in the philosophico-theological teaching of Thomas

Aquinas the notions of death, immortality of the soul, and resurrection are linked with one another. Naturally, the accent is going to lie on the philosophical aspect of the discussion.

8

To begin with: a word about the concept of "immortality of the soul," which, without any misgivings, we completely take for granted as a fundamental idea in Plato and which, with regard to its meaning, we think is hardly in need of special clarification. If we ask the question, *whose* immortality we can meaningfully speak about, it emerges (and indeed on the basis of a constraint incorporated in our living language itself which we can only evade by being caught up in the realm of the non-committal and the unreal) that, in exact and proper word usage, it can only be said of a living someone that he is immortal, just as it can only be said of a living someone that he dies. It will be seen that it is uncharacteristic of *Thomas* to speak of the "immortality of the soul." He always speaks of the intransitoriness and *incorruptibility* of the soul, while, like the New Testament, he attributes the name "immortality" to Christ, to the person in paradise, and the person who will in the future rise from the dead.– Now, however, if we have become accustomed, with regard to Plato, to speak of the "immortality of the soul," we are used to making the following link: that in Plato's view the soul is what gives the body its life and really constitutes the person and is only by chance and almost illegitimately yoked together with matter; and when this yoke is broken in death the real, true person lives on as immortal. Undoubtedly, this notion fits in with much that Plato says; but there is also much that does *not* fit. And precisely this lack of clear definition in Plato's concept of immortality is, I think, the exciting element and the one that opens up the subject more profoundly. In *Phaedrus*, one of the great late dialogues, the question is explicitly posed: "In what sense is a living thing called mortal or immortal – this we must try to clarify." And in this "attempt at clarification" he is no longer talking about *just the soul.* I quote: "We have in mind the image of a living being that is at one and the same time soul *and* body, both, however, grown together forever. But that is only one element of the concept of immortality presented in *Phaedrus*; the second element is the explicit connection with the *divine* sphere. He says, we think of immortality not as a concept belonging to reason – one that could be demonstrated – but we think of it in relation to the *gods*, "although we have not seen god nor do we have any adequate knowledge of him." Clearly, Plato's words and thoughts about immortality are interwoven with general Greek language usage, according to which men are simply "mortals" and the gods the "immortals." Erwin Rohde says: "When the Greeks say 'immortal' they are saying 'god': the two concepts are interchangeable."

9

Now the attempt must be made to say in a few theses what Plato thought about the life of the soul after death. I would like to formulate five such theses.

First, in Plato's work there is no rational speculation about what there is after death. Plato explicitly lays no claim to any kind of knowledge on this subject. Everything that is said in Plato's dialogues about the other world is taken from knowledge, one of the essential characteristics of which is that Plato himself is not its author. – This knowledge could be called "mythical" if the concept of myth were not so ambiguous. It is customary to use the general term "Platonic myths" not just to refer to Plato's stories about the gods. The term is also applied to every kind of illustrative parable that Plato uses. But, with regard to the binding nature of such stories, Plato makes important distinctions. Stories about the gods are handed down, about which Socrates, when asked whether he thinks they are true or false, says that he has more important things to do than to bother himself about them. But for him there is also "holy tradition" in the strict sense, the truth of which – no matter how difficult it may be to decipher – is inviolable; he considers it as knowledge coming down from a divine source. It is simply superior to all other human discourse. It is also not attainable by *ratio* – by argument and discussion – ; it is accessible only to those who are "wise in divine things." However we are to conceive of those gifted with such wisdom – Plato names priests and priestesses (the name Diotima comes to mind); he also names divinely inspired poets – neither Socrates nor Plato counts himself amongst them. It is myth in this special sense, this "holy tradition," this knowledge from a supra-human source with a claim to inviolable truth to which Plato explicitly has recourse in all he says about life after death. If this is overlooked or concealed (as, for example, in Mendelssohn's *Phaedo* where the extensive mythical narration of the judging of the dead is simply omitted), then not only is something decisive left out, but what remains is falsified. The melody of the whole is changed.

Second, the continued existence of the soul does not, according to Plato's explicit opinion, already imply anything that makes life after death the subject of human hope. Plato would never, as Kant puts it, see in the "infinitely continued existence of the rational being (which we call the immortality of the soul)" anything that would allow man to go confidently into death. Immortality as such, for him, precisely does *not* mean "eternal life." For the one who does not will the good, immortality means rather "a terrible danger."

Third, although Plato, with many explicit words, understands bodily man as the soul imprisoned in the body, strangely he understands, just as much, that dying is not the simple exit of the soul into freedom – a simple transition. The talk, presumed to be an interpretation of Plato, about death not being real (life in the other world is "only a simple continuation of life on earth insofar as this has a spiritual character," an "untroubled carrying on" – to use Thielicke's more drastic expression) – such talk has no relevance to Plato. This is indeed surprising. We really ought to expect something of this kind. But Socrates says expressly, and even with a positively polemic emphasis, that there *is* the opinion that the path leading to Hades is easy to tread, but that he is convinced that the transition of the soul into that other world is difficult and full of dangers. And then he gives his reason for this conviction – and here something comes to light that in no way seems to fit the image of Socrates, of whom Hegel says he alone of all the Athenians did not have himself initiated into the mysteries, because he "well knew that science and art do not originate from the mysteries and that wisdom is never contained in secrecy." In the *Phaedo* dialogue this same Socrates says: *that the soul's path into the world on the other side of death is not easy to tread he sees from what we do in death* ceremonies. The soul needs to be led; and thus tradition says that the same daimon that has protected man during his life also leads his soul on the path into the other world.

Fourth, this world and the other world are, in Plato's opinion, separated not just as a result of the separation of body and soul but by the judgment. For Plato there is simply no form of existence in the afterlife that does not result from a divine judicial decision. Judgment is passed on the life that has been lived, and its ultimate meaning is revealed and absolutely settled in the judgment. However manifold the images that are used in the myths related by Plato for describing life after death, one particular one is completely unambiguous: it is a life that happens to the soul and is allotted *by the gods*, deriving from their independent sovereignty.

Fifth, it is Plato's conviction that, on the basis of such judicial decisions, there are three forms of life after death. – Those who (as we read in *Phaedo*) have been found to be beyond curing because of the gravity of their offences plunge into Tartarus, "from whence they never again emerge." – In a radio talk in 1957 on the subject "Are we Immortal," Karl Barth speaks of the isolation of the person who is opposed to god and has succumbed to eternal death, and he adds: "Plato did not express it like this, nor has many another serious and deep thinker." My question is whether the *Phaedo* does not show that Plato does say exactly this! – The second form of afterlife is given to those who have led an average life and have therefore committed offences but yet are curable. They are brought to a place where they "do penance" and "purify themselves." To speak here of a "place of purification" is simply to use Plato's own words. – It remains to say, finally, how Plato describes life in the other world for the good and the just, what he means, in other words, by "eternal life." The just, he says, go up to that "pure dwelling place," of which it is further said that it contains sanctuaries in which not just images of the gods are found but in which the gods themselves truly dwell, so that a real *synousia*, a dwelling together of gods and men comes about.

10

Naturally it would be absurd to claim that with these theses the whole extent of Plato's teaching on death and immortality was even mapped out. To realize this one has only to consider what, as yet, has not been mentioned at all: the arguments for the indestructibility of the soul have, as I have said, been entirely left aside; nothing has been said about the fact that Plato's concept of immortality also includes the dimension of the past (the soul has "un-become"); the difficult theme of "transmigration of souls" has not been mentioned (here, by the way, I would say with Paul Friedländer that "Plato had *no* doctrine to do with transmigration of souls"). Yet the five theses I have formulated contain a fundamental correction of some broadly accepted false notions about Plato's thoughts regarding the continued life of the soul – notions which feed off many sources. If one accepts this corrective, one has, I think, admitted that at least the following ways of characterizing Plato's teaching *cannot* be maintained. First, one can no longer say that in Plato's view the continued life of the soul can be adequately described purely as a continued existence into infinity on the basis of our own natural powers. Second, it cannot further be maintained that the "Greek" teaching about the continued existence of the soul is a purely philosophical teaching in the sense that it is based exclusively on empirical knowledge and the *ratio*. At least this is not Plato's understanding. Here a new question arises which leads us into the sphere of the incalculable, namely, how are we to define, and what reality and what dignity adheres to, that which, leaving aside the empirical and the *ratio*, forms the foundation of Plato's teaching? Against the background of this question one final conclusion finds its special significance: namely, that it is scarcely possible still to maintain that the "Greek" and the Christian notion of what happens to the human soul after death have simply nothing to do with one another. In this one can agree with Oscar Cullmann when he says "(St) Paul certainly met people who could not accept his teaching about the resurrection precisely because they" (in Plato's sense) "believed in the immortality of the soul."

11

The following section of our discussion focuses on a particular *Christian* formulation of the relationship between death, immortality and resurrection, namely the formulation which is found in the work of Thomas Aquinas and, in the realm of Catholicism, has a certain representative significance.

If what happens in death can aptly be designated as a "separation of body and soul," the thinking about death is necessarily determined by how one understands the relationship, in the living person, between body and soul. For someone who believes that body and soul are two completely rounded realities in themselves death has to be something entirely different from what it means for someone who understands body and soul to be intrinsically related parts of one living real being. Plato is, again, representative of the first conception. His ideas are followed, even today, as models for thinking about death: soul and body are related to one another like the guest in the house that accommodates him; like the prisoner in jail; like the boatman in his boat. One particular notion has remained especially influential for thousands of years. It is found in the Alcibiades dialogue and says that the soul makes use of the body as a tool. Gilson says that all Christian thinkers *down to Thomas* shared this opinion, which came down from Plato through Plotinus and Augustine: *man is a soul that uses a body; homo . . . anima utens corpore.* Thomas himself will enforce another view which was also formulated in ancient philosophy – by Aristotle – that man, in reality, is not the soul that uses the body but the living unity made up of body and soul. This means that not only the human person has a bodily aspect, but the soul itself also has a bodily aspect. The soul, by its very nature – and this is what makes it to be soul – is what gives the body its essential form: *anima forma corporis.* The soul does "not possess the perfection of its own nature except in union with the body" – for which reason we have to say: not the soul separated from the body, not the "purely spiritual" soul, but the soul united with the body is more similar to God, even though God is non-corporeal. That is a formulation which clearly, though not expressly, envisages the resurrection of the body; and one is justified in assuming that Thomas, in his philosophical anthropology – far from establishing pure "Aristotelianism" – is in fact influenced by this article of faith, just as it has rightly been said that he would hardly have dared to take the idea of the unity in being of body and soul to its ultimate conclusion, and to uphold it, if he had not felt supported and encouraged by his faith in the truth of the Incarnation.

In any case, if one takes the relationship between body and soul in the living person to mean that both, together, constitute the one bodily person and that both are by nature intrinsically related, then it is *eo ipso* no longer possible to interpret death as an event that could leave any aspect of existence untouched: death affects the *whole* human person. And if one still must be able to maintain the indestructibility of the soul, this cannot be done in the sense that this part of ourselves simply continues to exist – "simply," meaning: as if death had not affected the soul, as if death had passed by and spared the soul. The separation of body and soul does not mean that "two" things until now joined together are separated from one another (the boat man disembarks), but rather: "one" thing, the human person as a bodily being, ceases to exist, *desinit esse actu.* If being human comes about through body and soul being one, then the separation of body and soul means the end of the real human being. Whatever might remain in being after death and beyond, it cannot be called "man" in the complete and exact sense of the word! – It is obvious that, in this, Thomas has made it very difficult for himself to answer the question as to how the soul is now still to be thought of as indestructible. But clearly he is not primarily concerned with avoidance of such theoretical problems.

12

As I have already said, Thomas does not at all speak of the "immortality" of the soul but of its indestructibility and incorruptibility (*incorruptibilitas*). By this is meant that the soul is such that it can neither be destroyed by any outside influence nor disintegrate and fade away through any weakening of its own strength. The question is: what does this *incorruptibilitas* exactly mean? Thomas defines it as follows: *Corruptibile est quod potest non esse; incorruptibile autem quod non potest non esse:* incorruptible is what is not capable of not being. Clearly, this can have very different meanings. And I think it needs further precise definition, mainly because, for example in the anthropology of idealism, the formulation has been understood literally in a sense that Thomas precisely did *not* mean. When Spinoza says *"Mens nostra aeterna est"* (our mind is eternal), or when Goethe says that the human mind is "something which by its nature is indestructible": it "continues its influence from eternity to eternity" – here an incorruptibility is being asserted which a Christian cannot possibly maintain because it presupposes that man is an absolute. The idealist type of such absoluteness (for example, the Fichtean kind: "that which is called death cannot break off my work . . . I have embraced eternity . . . when the last mote of the body that I call mine is destroyed, my will alone . . . must hover, daring and cool, over the rubble of the universe" – one must recall sometimes such a formulation!) – such a mode of thinking has been completely left behind; but I am convinced that there is much in contemporary existentialism that is only the painful and despairing form of that same idealism with regard to human autonomy. Even the disappointment is based on the conviction that that about which one is disappointed *ought to be* – while the Christian cannot be disappointed that man is not God. When, for instance, Sartre says: "It is absurd that we are born, and it is absurd that we die" one would like to answer him: what did you really expect? Did you expect that the existence of man has to have meaning of itself, be simply necessary, "incapable of not being" – as is the case with God alone? *Non potens non esse*: this is again quoting Thomas, but that cannot be what Thomas means by the *incorruptibilitas animae*. For Thomas the indestructibility of the soul means neither that the soul has existence in its own right nor that it can keep itself in existence by its own power. Of course, it also does not mean that, on the basis of its own nature, it is simply impossible for the soul to sink back into nothingness and to disappear completely out of reality – although it is, on the other hand, completely unthinkable that man could make this step of his own accord. That would presuppose what is, strictly speaking, creative – and therefore divine – power, the same that would be required to keep oneself in existence. (Here the common root of idealistic and nihilistic anthropology is identified.)

All of this means, first, that, when Thomas ascribes to the soul the impossibility of not being, he of course does not mean the power to be that could not be reconciled with the nature of man as creature. It is true that the specific nature of this *incorruptibilitas* has not yet been defined, and yet something important has been said, and by no means something purely negative. There is something positive, for example, in that the human soul possesses at least the kind of stability that belongs to created things as such, insofar as they are brought into being by God's creative will and cannot, by any kind of force, be reduced to nothingness – except by God himself. But, as Thomas says quoting the Book of Wisdom (1,14), God "has 'created all things for them to be' – and not so that they would sink into nothingness." No creature can be called simply transitory, *simpliciter corruptibilis* – as we read in the commentary to the *Sententiae* ("*Nothing* will be completely reduced to nothingness"; "all of God's works will remain in being for eternity – either as themselves or in their causes."). It would not be possible, from this starting point, to agree with the following statement of Karl Barth: man's mortality means that he exists within but not outside the time allotted to him: just as he did not exist beforehand, so he will not exist afterwards. Can one maintain this when "beforehand" means before creation?

By the specific indestructibility of the human soul Thomas means something more than, and different from, that general continuity in being of creation as a whole. He means that, although the whole human person dies, the soul is not merely intransitory "in its causes" – i.e., in some sort of elements and fundamental forces belonging to some all-embracing entity – but that it, as itself, *secundum se*, remains indestructibly in being beyond death, and this by virtue of the *nature* of the soul. For Thomas, the term "by virtue of its nature" always amounts to the same as saying "by virtue of creation" – and so he would never accept the designation "absolute immortality" as applicable to the *incorruptibilitas* he upholds (although such a designation is sometimes used polemically in Evangelical theology). *But*: precisely on the basis of his conception of creation, which says that God, by creating, really communicates being, i.e. does not retain it for himself but gives it to the *creature*, so that the creature now possesses it as its own real property – precisely on the basis of this concept of creation Thomas would insist that intransitoriness is something that belongs to the soul itself because of what the soul, by its very nature, *is*. But this seems to be exactly what Paul Althaus means by the expression "absolute immortality." The Christian faith only knows, he says, an immortality based on God's will, but not an "absolute" immortality, for which reason Christian faith cannot allow of an "immortality that stems from the nature of the soul." Of course, Thomas is also convinced that there is a God-given immortality – that of the human person in paradise and that of the person raised from the dead – which is not already given in the nature of the soul; and I said already: only this kind of immortality of the *whole* person is for Thomas immortality in the strict sense. But he would never give up the idea that the soul has a natural intransitoriness based in its own being, and of this he would say it is *eo ipso* "based on God's will." To see this and keep it in mind seems to me, in this context, of greater importance for an understanding of St. Thomas's teaching on immortality than a critical discussion of the individual arguments, amongst which also the Platonic arguments are preserved and confirmed. These arguments essentially amount to saying that the soul, despite its dependence on the body, is seen to be – above all through its capacity for truth – in the end an immaterial, simple entity which is superior to the body and *for that reason* can be considered as having its own individual intransitoriness.

13

It is doubtless not easy to think of the indestructibility of the soul together with what Thomas says about death as the end of real person. And he says it on numerous occasions with almost brutal emphasis that, whatever it is that remains after death, it cannot strictly be called "man" (Mensch). For example, he says that it is not possible, strictly speaking, to call the hand of the dead person a hand. – But then, as far as the condition of the departed "soul" is concerned, Thomas – apart from the statement of very general and hypothetical characteristics – is just as reticent as the New Testament. He takes up the biblical image of "sleeping peacefully" in his own typical way: just as those who are asleep or in some other way are transported from their body, so the departed soul is, in a more intense way, open and receptive to the influence of higher powers. What Thomas insists on is that the soul, when separated from the body, is *not* the human being (der Mensch); it is *not* "person." The *anima separata*, being a part separated from the whole, finds itself in a state that is not only imperfect but one that is necessarily repugnant to nature. He says this many times.

The conclusion to be drawn is: because final happiness is also the *perfection* of the blessed themselves, man cannot reach his ultimate happiness unless the soul is again united with the body; furthermore, since a state that is repugnant to nature cannot endure, "the immortality of souls seems to demand the future resurrection of the bodies." Formulations of this kind, it seems, can only be taken to mean that future resurrection is fundamentally only a form of restoration of the natural order. While this interpretation is, in fact, in line with Thomas's opinion, it would fail to grasp the core of his statement and would obscure it. It would pass over the fact that, for Thomas, resurrection at the end of time can only be understood as the vanquishing of death through Christ alone – a completely miraculous, strictly supernatural event brought about by grace. It is in no way caused by any power in human nature but purely as a direct divine

intervention (*sola virtute divina*). It is an event, furthermore, of which even the most profound human thought
and sounding can give us no knowledge or certainty. We
can only know about it through divine revelation, i.e.
through faith. But now: (*suppositis his*), presupposing that
this is the case, an additional supporting rational argument – an *evidens ratio* – becomes valid as a proof of the
future resurrection of the flesh, *ad ostendendam resurrec-
tionem carnis futuram*. This proof is the argument used
just now that takes its weight from the philosophical
teaching that man is by nature a living unity of body and
soul (*anima forma corporis, corpus anima formatum*).
Thomas is saying here that, because the indestructible
spiritual soul – by virtue of its very nature – remains ori-
ented to the body even after death, there is, in the constitution of natural man's being, an aptitude (*aptitudo*) for
that physical immortality (future immortality as well as
the original immortality in paradise), although this aptitude can find its fulfillment (*complementum*) not through
any natural power but only through supernatural intervention. And so it may seem offensive and open to misinterpretation – but it is not at all an inaccurate use of language – when Thomas refers to the resurrection in a certain sense as "natural": "Resurrection is natural with
regard to its result (*finis*), insofar as it is natural for the
soul to be united to the body, whereas its cause (*principium ejus activum*) is not natural; it is, instead, brought
about solely through divine power." Thomas illustrates
his meaning by using the example of the miraculous
healing of the blind man: the outcome, sight, is something natural, whereas the force that restores the sight is
something beyond nature. To the question whether
God's supernatural intervention is limited to achieving

something that is also within the range of human possibilities, Thomas would probably say, amongst other things: that for Holy Scripture resurrection and immortality are not simply the same as salvation and eternal life.

14

I must again close this short overview by saying what important points in the teaching of St. Thomas have, of necessity, not been dealt with. Apart from a few brief comments, nothing has been said about the individual philosophical arguments for the intransitoriness of the soul; the question about the sense in which death is "natural" and the sense in which it is "punishment" has not been discussed; and nothing has been said about the ending of the *status viatoris* that takes place in death.

My main aim was to make two things clear: first, how in Thomas's theological (i.e. insofar as it is based on revelation) teaching about death, immortality and resurrection, the philosophical (i.e. gained in the encounter with experienced reality) interpretation of natural man holds firm – though admittedly it is incomplete and anything but conclusive; second, that this linking of philosophical and theological thought is based on the conviction that God's creative activity and the working of His divine grace proceed from the same source, and that what comes from creation, from nature, is the presupposition and foundation for *everything* that may be given to the creature as an additional divine gift. Thomas in no way thinks that the true overcoming of death lies in the natural indestructibility of the spiritual soul. But he does think that, if the human soul were not immortal by virtue of creation, there would be nothing and nobody to *receive* the divine gift of resurrection and eternal life.

Of course, for Thomas this conviction is not a philosophical but a theological one based on the interpretation of revelation. And it makes the controversial theological discussion particularly difficult that, on the basis of this theological conviction, he already incorporates the documents of revelation in his thinking – for which reason, for example, he can say, quite in contrast to the thesis proposed at the beginning of our discussion: "in Holy Scripture there are innumerable (*infinitae*) testimonies to the immortality of the soul."

Doing and Signifying

Contemporary man, or, more exactly, the person existing today in European civilized society the world over, is becoming ever less capable, it seems, of understanding how an action that is not aimed at a directly practical effect could have any meaning at all. And anyone who would undertake to observe the physical behavior, in public, of an active man would hardly have the occasion to see such an action. When Christopher Columbus penetrated into the interior of the island of Cuba, the natives put a stalk across the entrance of their huts to protect themselves against the foreign warriors. This, from a practical point of view, ineffective and in fact non-existent barrier, was, of course, just as easy to break through then as it would be today. But Columbus gave the order to respect the symbolic barrier. Such respect and, even more so, such trust have in the meantime become somewhat improbable. – But we do not need to have recourse to such distant examples. Only fifty years ago the observer of human behaviour could not have missed the expansive gesture with which people greeted one another – a gesture which equally was not meant to achieve anything but to express, display, and mean something: namely, respect, *reverentia* for another. In modern big cities one will hardly ever see anything of this kind: instead, a curt word of greeting, a nod of the head perhaps accompanied by an economical, quick gesture with the hand. Such shriveled forms of greeting, as we know, have been for a long time becoming established as general practice. It seems we are in agreement with this, we have nothing against it, we find it acceptable that things are a bit more sober and scant, at least "out there" in the street and in the market place. At least the *public* forms of expression should be, we feel, as "objective" as possible, practical, serving a purpose – and nothing besides.

The question now, of course, is whether any danger lurks in this attitude, the danger, namely, that it will be established where it is not only not appropriate but even destructive – for example in the sphere of eros or religious cult. – If the eye of the imaginary observer were to penetrate the walls of a nearby church he would doubtless see not just a few gestures that first and foremost are meant to mean something: the blessing; kneeling; folded hands; lights which are kindled not for illumination of the space but as witness to dedication of the heart; bread that one eats not to satisfy physical hunger but to partake of God's life. Human actions of this kind still continue, in fact, to happen – no differently today than fifty or a thousand years ago. The only question is how relevant or how strange they seem in the middle of the modern world of work. Is it at all possible to expect that contemporary man can readily understand such things? Probably the answer is "no." It cannot be expected. But this statement should not, from the beginning, have any connotation of criticism let alone accusation. If one is geared almost completely (and not at all because of the willfulness of the individual) to use the category of the practical and the useful, it is only natural that one finds it difficult to discover what kind of meaning there could be in actions that, strangely, are not meant to achieve something practical. Of course, this difficulty does not usually result in silent embarrassment. Often enough it is expressed in highly aggressive argument. And that is the point where the debate begins.

Three or four different opinions are distinguishable

at the outset. Although they can hardly be reduced to a common denominator, they are, as a whole, both close to and familiar to people of this time. – The first argument, perhaps the most plausible of them, is: it is of no conse-quence, one way or the other, if someone, for example, lights a candle in a church as a sign – as is said – of his inner dedication to God. Is this dedication itself not the only thing that matters? Either one has it – and then the candle is superfluous; or one does not have it – and then it is meaningless: a sign for something that does not exist! And, generally speaking, why have a visible gesture at all (laying on of hands, eating, drinking, candles) if what is really important is the invisible?

A *second* voice sounds like this: realistically, that which is romantically called the "self-consuming flame" is nothing more than an instance of a simple process of burning: a purely material, chemical process. And what could that have to do with dedication, sacrifice, love?

A *third* view introduces an entirely different thought: our world today has already, because of the rule of expe-diency, become barren, ugly and impoverished enough, so that we should, in every way, preserve the rich forms and pure beauty of traditional customs if only for the sake of memory.

There is still a *fourth* view to be considered. But the peculiar thing here is that, while it has been emphatical-ly cherished from time immemorial and is so even today, the modern person will hardly dare to say it out loud –perhaps even to himself. Put succinctly: sometimes, in certain extreme situations when it is, so to speak, a mat-ter of life and death, all that is important is the visible, physical sign; conviction, opinion, thought are then com-pletely indifferent; the only thing that "helps" is a particular, simply spoken word, a clear gesture, or even a candle lit in a consecrated place.

For my part, I would continue the debate by saying that none of these four theses goes to the heart of the matter. And I believe that this can be shown, point for point. So, point *one*: of course it is right to say that the inner attitude is the important thing. But we are not made in such a way that something concerning the living person can at the same time be "purely inward," or "purely spiritual"; on the contrary: in normal circumstances, what is inward expresses itself outwardly, and the spiritual takes on a bodily shape. – The opposite side of the coin, however, is (point *two*): nothing human is "purely material." While I can, for example, describe human speech as a physiological or acoustic process or as quantity of ink put on paper in certain geometric forms, I still have not grasped what is peculiar to word and language. Naturally, burning a candle is a material process; but as soon as this chemical process becomes an element of a human utterance it takes on something of the character of a word; but no one understands a word if he ignores the spiritual, the non-material aspect of it. Neither he nor the other person who only acknowledges the inner aspect, the inner attitude – the invisible, spiritual element – has access to an understanding of the *symbol*, the nature of which is to be the visible form of the invisible. But that is a defect which has an acute bearing on life. If one separates the visible from the invisible one is made incapable of understanding symbols. It is not just a question of candles and stalks or individual poetic and religious symbols. It is a question of understanding or not understanding, of realizing or not realizing a whole dimension of live human existence. – The purely aesthetical evaluation (point *three*) adds nothing here. To think it does is dangerous self-deception of a kind that is wide-spread amongst contemporary intellectuals. It is true, the world becomes a wilderness, a desert where expediency rules as soon as symbols disappear. But when one tries to preserve symbols purely because of their colorful and interesting charm, one is undertaking something which is hopeless from the start – because in doing this, though perhaps in an intellectually stimulating way, one is not taking symbols seriously. – By comparison (point *four*), the final thesis mentioned can be referred to as almost "primitive" – which does not mean that it is foreign to intellectuals or that it is easy to make a judgment about it or to dismiss it. We are dealing with the age-old, ineradicable notion of *magic*. Magic is based on mistaking effect for meaning. To light a candle, to touch a sacred image, to make the sign of the cross – these are believed to be actions with direct effect, like the turning on of a water tap, a blow with the fist, the opening of a door. Yet it must be admitted that even here there is a grain of truth; more precisely, we have a feeling, a sense of something that is – unbelievably – real. Something further has to be said about this.

But first it is important to see that, naturally, an understanding of symbol and a realization of symbol cannot flourish particularly well in such soil – namely, in an atmosphere of pure expediency and in an atmosphere, moreover, which is affected by a spiritualistic or materialistic misinterpretation of reality, by aesthetic and museum-like resignation or the hidden virulence of magic. – But where there is no place for symbol many other things normally come under threat, and that need not surprise us. Literature, for example, must become questionable, like all the other arts; likewise the philosopher's relationship to the world; but, above all, religious ceremonies.

At this point of the debate I prepare myself for the following critical and perhaps also impatient objection: that is all very true, but it is based on a false premise and for that reason is, strictly speaking, also *not* true. That modern man has become increasingly incapable of understanding symbols and that he is ever less inclined actively to use them – this fact cannot be denied. Perhaps it is to be deplored. But in any case it is inevitable and for that reason it is basically meaningful. What is the point in lamenting that a price has to be paid for exploitation of nature through technology which ultimately makes it possible that we survive at all! When we become used to field glasses, compasses, and radar, naturally we lose the Indians' infallible intuition. Clearly we cannot enjoy the benefits of technical civilization and still retain the primitive tracker's sure instincts. Wanting to have both together is pure fantasy and lack of sobriety. Do we not simply have to take into account that humanity is undergoing change? Modern man has no other choice than, in an enormous effort aimed exclusively at practical ends, to harness the forces of nature to his service. Is it, then, not simply acceptable that the sense for the *other* kind of activity is more and more lost to him – for precisely that kind of activity which primarily does not effect anything but is meant to mean something?

That is a precise and weighty objection to which there is no easy reply. To a large extent it is justified. We do, indeed, have to pay for the technical civilization of which we enjoy the benefits – amongst other things, by a loss of understanding of the symbolical. But here, of course, the question arises of when the price is beyond our means.

Put plainly: where is the boundary beyond which we are no longer speaking merely of a "changing" humanity but only of dehumanizing, degeneration, inhumanity? We have already been prepared for the time, in the not too distant future, when certain "poetic" forms of writing will no longer exist. It is not a question of "poesie," says T.S. Eliot. It has long since been clear that the era of the comprehensive speculative philosophical systems is past. All of that, it seems to me, is something we can bear and cope with. Perhaps it is something, strictly speaking, which does not amount to a real loss. It is probable, furthermore, that certain "barock" forms of divine worship are less and less viable, even unbearable, for contemporary people – even Christians. That, too, I think, we can bear without any loss of substance. Certainly, also, in the religious sphere more than anywhere else, the impassable borderline we have mentioned is clearly seen. Existence becomes obviously inhuman as soon as in that sphere there is, on principle, no longer any room for any kind of "sacred rite" (an idea which cannot properly be seen as unreal fantasy). By "sacred rite" I do not mean here just any kind of particular act of worship – whether Christian, Islamic, or Hindu. I am referring to what is common to all of these concrete forms: namely, that the honoring of an absolute divine power takes place in visible forms that appeal to the senses. Perhaps someone will ask what that has to do with our theme "symbol" and "the understanding of symbols." The answer is: neither with any primitive people nor in the great cultures of the Far East, neither in European antiquity nor with Christians of this century is there any kind of sacred action that is not symbolic. We are unable to imagine it being otherwise. But that means: anyone whose sense of symbol has been lost and has died out would not be able to understand or perform a sacred rite. And at this point the borderline would undoubtedly have been crossed. Whether an existence without literature, without any trace of the artistic, without philosophy – i.e. without a thought that concerns the totality of the world – could still truly be called "human" – perhaps we could, in this regard, be left in some doubt. But through the complete absence, and even more so through the fundamental impossibility of a "sacred rite" – through such a loss existence becomes obviously and necessarily inhuman. It should be possible to make this clear to anyone with an open mind. But even this would not reveal to him what is really bad in this respect.

In every symbolic action we have spoken of so far, whether literary or sacred, it has always been a question of signs which *we* create, signs which we give. But is it not possible that a sign is *given to us*, a sign from elsewhere, the deciphering and interpretation of which is expected of us (expected of, entrusted to, required of, permitted to – however you see it)? Could not the improbable happen, something that in fact is almost unbelievable, even miraculous (it comes to the same thing; the concept of the miraculous is that something absolutely extraordinary happens, something inexplicable, something that reason finds alarmingly incomprehensible) – could it not possibly happen that *God* would give us a sign, a sign that likewise is visible to the senses (otherwise we could not perceive it at all)? Such a sign would naturally be infinitely superior to all the signs and symbols that *we* can produce; more precisely, it would achieve what magic senses as an ultimate possibility but strives in vain to produce. Because it would be a divine, a creator's sign – in the fullest sense creative – it would not, like our signs, merely "signify" something, but it would at the same time "do" what it signifies.

In saying this I have, without realizing it, used almost the exact formulation which Christian theology employs to define a sacrament. Christianity is based, in fact, on the supposition – or rather, on the belief – that God has really given and continues to give signs of this kind – above all in nourishment through sacred bread by which man partakes not only of divine gifts but of God himself. One can only expect that, for the non-Christian, these things are completely unthinkable, unbelievable. But, again, this is exactly what is said in theology: we are dealing with something, the root of which lies in a reality that is not accessible to us by natural means. But it is not my place, as a non-theologian – and it is not my intention – to go into this any further. Only one thing concerns me: to make something more plausible, even for the non-Christian, namely: that, *should* God, unbelievably, in fact have given man such signs, no one who has become deaf to the language of symbol can understand and thereby enjoy the fruit of these signs which are so important for life and are so salutary. *That* is the extremely dire situation we need to consider here. No one can "truly *enjoy* a sacrament – and it is given to be enjoyed – if his sense for the symbolic and the sacramental has not been nourished." This sentence, though one would not immediately guess it, stems from Goethe's amazing section in *Poetry and Truth* (Dichtung und Wahrheit) dedicated to the seven sacraments. He clearly makes the point that the symbolic sense is also the sacramental sense, and that its loss is unthinkable because it would result in man becoming incapable of achieving what is the highest and most essentially human thing: namely, to experience and to receive whatever invisible gift God has given him in a (visible) earthly form.

A question already posed at the beginning now seems, after all that, even more difficult to answer: the question about the *public sphere*. Precisely someone who accepts the above arguments could say, for example: because, in the symbolic gesture, especially in the sacramental religious gesture, the most intimate, personal side of the human person is exposed – unprotected and defenseless, so to speak – it needs, for this very reason, the safety of a *non*-public space which is open only to the initiated. Perhaps, very much from a distance, we may admire the untroubled attitude of the devout Moslem who spreads out his carpet in the street and bows in the direction of Mecca. But, basically, that remains very foreign to us and we know that we are justified in feeling that it is impossible to make the gesture of prayer in public, in the presence of casual witnesses who do not belong. And so, is it not completely understandable that within our European civilization, the symbolic sacramental rites have, since the Middle Ages, with more and more reason been withdrawn from the public gaze and carried out in the seclusion of a closed sacred space? What can be said against that?

There is no simple, straightforward answer to that. It is true that "being in the public eye" today refers above all to the sphere of mass reactions, which means the place of celebratory self-surrender of the individual, the place of mindless joining in, the place where loud volume and quantity exercise their naked power. It is, furthermore, the place of unbridled curiosity, of curiosity nourished by endless boredom and armed with the powerful instruments of technology, a curiosity which demands to see everything without being a real part of it and which, strictly speaking, does not want awareness but only wants to see. And, finally, this public sphere is the hunting-ground for interested parties and business; there is nothing public that is not "of interest to the market"! – *Everything* that exposes itself to the "light of the public realm" unavoidably enters this force field. For this reason it seems highly desirable and necessary to put a wall around the place for sacred rites and to shield it against the noisy profanity of the public arena. I understand very well what a friend recently posed for consideration: the monstrance with the host on the advertising boards of airline companies almost made him question the sacrament itself. True, so much can be said. But against this: "profane" is not simply the same as "public." Profane is only what is precisely un-holy; the "world" as a perversion of creation; human society insofar as it turns away from God. Only a degenerate public sphere is profane. On the other hand, a sacred rite is, of its very nature, not a private or secret thing. By virtue of its nature it is a *public* act; its symbolism reaches beyond the world of men. It includes the whole cosmos, so that we have to say: the sacred rite in which not only we ourselves give signs (signs of honor and devotion) but in which, much more, the God-given sacramental signs – when we carry them out – have the effect on us of what they signify: purification, consolation, nourishment, salvation beyond all that can be named and comprehended – this sacred rite is performed in the midst of the world; its scene and its place of operation is creation as a whole. One can hardly think of anything that is less exclusive, less capable of containment, or more geared to comprehensive publicity, more

96

demanding of a public – naturally, one which is appropriate and non-profane!

And so, because the sacred rite requires the participation of appropriate people and a publicity from which no one is excluded; because it has to be protected against profanation, but also against exclusiveness; because all of these warring elements simultaneously retain their value and position – for that very reason, as I have said, there can be no single-stranded handy answer available in this matter.

A fitting answer would, however, have to contain the following: that a view of the sacred rite should be accessible – from time to time; seldom, but then untheatrically – even to a degenerate, secularized, profane public. It is possible, even probable, that this view would simply be submerged in the uninterrupted show of events, plays, and other attractions. It is also possible that it would shock, challenge, unsettle. But perhaps in favorable circumstances this sight could awaken a memory, a sense of the true order of things in the world.

"Consecration of the World"
In answer to a questionnaire

I

In the religious sphere it seems – just as in the philosophical and artistic spheres – that there is the particular danger that language will suddenly become a kind of jargon inviting us to a non-committal use of language which, while it poses as particularly "religious" or "philosophical" or "artistic" and is also deemed by many to be such, has in fact lost its direct connection with the original object in question. It has gone so far that our only recourse is to a conscious abstaining from language and to a determined insistence on that frank, sober language which is usually forced on us by our busy dealings with reality.

It would be bad if such a superb formulation as "Consecration of the World," *consecratio mundi,* should be enmeshed in the mill of such facile, non-committal use of language. There is already a hint of this danger, so that extreme sobriety and an almost aggressively realistic approach are required even in discussion about what is actually meant.

The bishop consecrates water or oil, so that now we have "holy water" and "holy oil"; the priest consecrates bread and wine, so that they are now, in a completely unique sense, "sacred nourishment." Clearly what happens here is that these natural things – water, oil, bread, wine – are brought into an entirely new relationship to divine reality. This is precisely what the consecration, the *consecratio,* consists in.

Now when we speak of the "consecration of the world" as of a human duty, this can only mean that the "world" is likewise to be brought into a new relationship with divine reality. The question is how one does this!

First: who can do it? In the case of "consecration" of water and oil or of bread and wine it is not man, whether priest or bishop, but God himself; it is the divine Logos who has become man that carries out the consecration.

A further question is: what is meant here by "the world"? If the quintessence of all created things is meant, the Christian, above all, is not allowed to forget that creation, *because* it is *creatura*, is – from the beginning, and of necessity – intimately close to God the Creator. Because the very existence of the creature implies being aroused by the divine *actus purus* – for that reason, according to Thomas Aquinas's understanding of the matter – everything created is not only "good" but is shot through with God; creation *is* "consecrated." How then should man be able to "consecrate" the world (as creation)? What he is able to do and is also required to do seems to be: to recall to mind and to respect as sacred the sacredness that adheres to creation by virtue of its being, which no human "improvement" or additional religious consecration can heighten or provide with a further foundation. But can that be called "consecration of the world"?

But probably "world" is taken to include *man* himself and *human things*: the world of work, politics, marriage and family, education, technology – and so on. "Consecration" of such a world could be achieved in two different forms: first, in our respect for the sacredness that is *in* those human things themselves, i.e. in the actual order of creation; second, by clearing the way for entry into our hearts – and into the shaping of our human world – of God's sanctifying influence as revealed in the incarnation of the Logos. And so *we* are not the consecrators of the world. What we are able and obliged to do is this: to make sure that the sanctification of the world by God's grace and by his creative force meets – in man's freedom – with as little resistance as possible and with the strongest possible acceptance and active affirmation.

II

For this task, *the layman as layman* seems to me to have some special possibilities. – First: the daily practical dealing with resistant reality, with the compact world of our direct experience, could enable the layman to take care, with great sensitivity, that speech about God and sacred things does not lose its clear link with actuality, its realistic commitment and sobriety. The much discussed layman's criticism of the average Sunday sermon seems to me to mean exactly this: that the religious vocabulary cannot be taken radically and seriously enough in its literal meaning. Theologians owe us laymen some answers – precisely with regard to the theme "consecration of the world." For example, every Christian knows what "really" (though in a mysterious way) happens in the sacraments or also in the blessing of the baptismal water. But what happens "really" when a parish or a diocese is "consecrated" to the heart of Mary? Apart from the prayer for protection, does anything really happen at all? What objective reality corresponds to the act by which Saint Clara is declared patroness of television broadcasting?

Second: it seems in a special way to fall to the layman to insist on respect for the sacredness of creation as found in the natural things of the world; to stand up for this sacredness and to defend it not only against a fundamentally irreverent, secularized abuse but also against the short circuit of a religiosity which is completely other-worldly and thinks it can bypass natural creation.

Third: the layman can, by his presence in all areas of life in the world, open the way to the sanctifying work of God (not only of the Creator but also of the God who reveals Himself in Christ). He can do this not only by an unspoken representation, i.e. through the simple fact of living like a Christian as a matter of course, but also through the spoken message. Both of these can be done in an endless variety of ways. Precisely the influence of the layman cannot have external norms imposed. For example, one can think of the case where an academic teacher avoids making a statement in the context of explicitly religious events in favor of the higher effect of *the* preaching which he achieves in his teaching practice, in a way that is appropriate to the subject he is treating. Here, no one but the lecturer himself is in a position to make a judgment about the method and the extent of this preaching. Here (and not in some sort of need for a status of equality) is the real reason that the responsible layman has to act, with complete independence, in his own sphere of influence.

III

Now when it is a question of pondering the "most suitable means" and "what reforms are required" I would like to sum up what I think is indispensable by using one word: "Arkan-Disziplin." I do not mean by this that the Church should withdraw into the sacristy or into the catacombs or start to behave like a secret sect. On the contrary, I think it is meaningful and necessary to utilize all the modern technical means of communication to help in carrying out the missionary task. But at the same time we must realize more deeply than heretofore that the "consecration of the world" cannot take place by means of a profanation of the sacred. Instead, the innermost sphere of the sacred, the divine mystery present in visible signs, has to be protected through consciously practiced silence, through a disciplined abstinence from "religious" terminology, through the definite refraining from show and publicity. This innermost sphere must remain reserved for the truly "sanctifying" celebration shared by the initiated. Everyone can belong here, but only on the basis of initiation.

Life of the Spirit
A meditation for Pentecost

Whenever one of the great traditional feasts of the year is to be celebrated we feel, whether we admit it or not, a certain embarrassment. We are at the same time tempted to let ourselves be convinced by a fine-sounding and good-natured general optimism that this is of no consequence. Yet something remains which refuses acceptance. And it would, indeed, not be good to let oneself be fully pacified, to ignore the problem, and to pass over it lightly.

But if one tries to offer resistance, goes ahead and looks at this embarrassment head-on, seeks clarity and tries to put a name on it, it soon becomes clear that two things have to be discussed which, while related to one another, are, however, not identical.

The first point is that we seem to have lost contact with the directly practical knowledge of how any feast is to be celebrated. As soon as the need to make a living no longer preoccupies us we don't know what to do: according to what we read in André Gide's diary, this is simply "the truth." He notes this not by way of complaint or accusation but with the calm frankness of a detached diagnostician. And who could deny that his statement exactly describes average reality – the way every person experiences it, for example, on waking up on the morning of a feast day.

Let us suppose that this person has no need to sleep any longer and has no correspondence to attend to. No, the only thing that has "to be done" is the celebration of the feast, this alone, but precisely this. Let us further suppose that this person has enough awareness and honesty not to allow himself any of the not quite unusual escapes. He has accepted that the communal drink, the banquet, the excursion into the countryside are not to be considered a sufficient and proper celebration of the feast – a welcome addition, a meaningful ornament, yes, but not the thing itself. But what is this thing itself? What does it mean to *celebrate* a feast day? How does one do it?

The embarrassment does not concern only *how* celebrations are performed. It derives from the fact that – and this is the second point – a live knowledge of the meaning of our great feast days is to a large extent missing. What is being celebrated at Christmas and Easter? Some recent fairly unsettling questionnaires have brought to light how clueless the average answers are – and what an odd and strange thing it is when these feast days are "held" just the same.

And now: what is celebrated at Pentecost, on the feast of the Spirit? If we try to say exactly what "Spirit" really is, we first of all think of its immaterial, bodiless aspect. The ancients, on the other hand, understood the spirit as the power to come into contact with the totality of the world. What distinguishes a spiritual being is that the sphere in which it lives is that of reality as a whole. The life of the spirit amounts, therefore, to existing face to face with the world as a whole: *vis-à-vis de l'univers.* Thus, spiritual life in the full sense of the word happens only where total reality is involved – which does not mean the totality of diverse *individual* things, but the overall meaning, the essential foundation of all that is.

But when do we come to be in touch with the totality in this way? Certainly not by focusing on the achievement of concrete goals, such as the aiming at "making a living" in the broadest sense of the word. However much intelligence, inventiveness, discipline and seriousness is naturally required here, none of the great witnesses of Western tradition – not Plato, not Aristotle, not Augustin, not Thomas – would have called this "spiritual life" (which in no way means that they would not have accorded their respect, even admiration, for the achievements of the technical man.) The diary entry of André Gide points not merely to the non-celebratory nature of an exclusively "practical" life but also to its dangerous proximity to the non-spirit. In a word, it becomes clear now that feast and spirit are interrelated in a special way.

But again: when do we make contact with the world in its totality? The answer: for example, when we think of signs which are presented to us in literature, music, and all the plastic arts. The meditation of the philosopher also concerns the totality of the world. But, above all, religious contemplation must be mentioned – the submersion of the self, in meditation, into the mysteries of God's word. – What this says is that these are the forms of truly spiritual life – because only in this way does the eye of the soul open to the most extreme possible level of receptiveness which alone can respond to the totality of the real.

Of course we are dealing with a reception, a hearing and keeping silent, an openness to experience and, accordingly, with something which is not so completely in our control as is the case with the more manly activity of the intellect that explores the world. And so the names by which human language seeks to grasp the essence of spirit, such as breath, storm, fountain, and flame – all of them say mainly this: spirit does not fit in with any directives of the human planner; it withdraws itself from anyone's arbitrary control; it blows where it will.

Naturally, all of that does not immediately refer to the "Spirit" we celebrate at Pentecost – and yet it is an image of the same. And how else could our understanding approach the "Holy Spirit" if not by using the more accessible images we have – treading, in this, the path which has always been trod? I will never be convinced that that very early voice from the sixth century BC which says: just as the breath of life in our body is the dominant force, so too the world as a whole is governed by breath, the *pneuma* – I will never accept the current thesis in the handbooks that what this voice means is the meteorological fact of air and atmosphere and not also, in some sense, the "Spirit of the Lord that fills the earth."

Of course, Christendom's sacred books are able to give much more profound information: it is not some sort of ruling force, but a someone, a personal spirit; not just a blowing and surging, but "Love" – another name that signifies a force beyond our control! And we are also told: man's own spirit cannot grasp the totality of the world more surely than when it lets itself be flooded by this divine force. And this only means that "spirituality" is the most extreme realization of the life of the spirit.

How, then, is the "Feast of the Spirit" to be celebrated? – It needs to be said here that two answers can be given: one esoteric and the other exoteric. And this, too, must be said: that this is not the place for the esoteric answer, i.e. for the Christian answer in the full sense. All that has been said so far only comes as far as the threshold.

But the embarrassment mentioned at the beginning, that each one of us keeps on experiencing, contains hope – if we are not too quick to be pacified. For who will say how near or how far the unspoken sigh of pain that expresses our puzzlement is from the "inexpressible sighs," of which it is said in the Scripture that they are produced by the Spirit itself?

The Theory of Virtues
as Statement about Man

The word used in modern languages to refer to the old concept *areté* (virtus) has to a large extent lost its freshness and also its impact. Max Scheler states, in his essay on "Rehabilitation of Virtue" written before World War I, that the word which in other times was used to refer to "a delightful, attractive and charming person" has since been so cast off "that we can hardly avoid smiling when we hear it or read it." Similarly, Paul Valéry said in a lecture to the *Académie Française* that the word *vertu* is dead and that this is seen, for example, in the fact that – apart from the academic context – the word is only used in operettas and in the catechism. It is doubtful whether this process, in which the meaning of the word disappears or is twisted, can be halted or even canceled. But that is less important, provided that what was originally meant by the word – the *concept* "virtue" which has now likewise become largely unrecognizable – can be brought back into general awareness. For an ethical theory of life this concept seems to be completely indispensable. At least in Western thinking about human morality the doctrine of virtue has been one of the fundamental forms in which the attempt has been made to give a systematic formulation of what man "should do."

Other basic forms which occur alongside the doctrine of virtue are, above all: the doctrines regarding the commandments, duties, and stages of development. The Christian doctrine regarding the commandments mainly takes the form of interpretation of the ten commandments; in the age of the Reformation a special "biblical" accent was given as a necessary corrective to the doctrine of virtue of medieval scholasticism, which was considered "Greek" and "philosophical."

The doctrine of duty is likewise a fundamental form developed since antiquity, especially amongst the Stoa. It derives its special importance – which is still influential in the present day – from the interpretation of St Paul, where he says that we "should live with reserve, justice, and piety in this world" (*Titus* 2,11ff.). Calvin uses this text as a basis for his division of the spheres of duty into three parts, which has an influence way beyond areas directly affected by Calvinism and is seen especially in the ethics of the Enlightenment: duties towards God (pious), duties towards one's neighbor (just), and duties regarding ourselves (reserve). – The doctrine of levels places the accent on the different levels a person has to go through, step by step, on the way to achieving moral perfection. "Ladder," "climax," "scale" are basic terms which characteristically recur. There seems to be a certain affinity between this form of ethical doctrine about life and religious mysticism. The notion of the ascent to the divine by steps is prominent both in Plato's doctrine of Eros and in Neoplatonic ethics. The formulation by Dionysius the Areopagita of their distinction of the three stages "purification – enlightenment – union" remains valid right down to the Spanish mysticism of the sixteenth century. The structure of the doctrine of levels is also typical for the early monks of the Christian East, for the theology of the Byzantine Middle Ages, and for the Western mystics (Bernhard of Clairvaux, Hugo of St. Victor, Bonaventure, Tauler, Seuse).

The doctrine of virtue came from the Greeks into the ethics of the West. Pythagoras already seems to have distinguished between the four cardinal virtues. In Plato's time the notion is taken for granted, so much so that, as the example of Agathon's speech in Plato's *Symposium* shows, the virtues provide the plan for an encomium. The *Nicomachean Ethics* of Aristotle, who defines the formal concept of virtue more precisely, contains the structure of the doctrine of virtue, although it is not exclusively based on the division into the four cardinal virtues. These appear more explicitly in the Stoa and are then once and for all named by Cicero in the order in which they are later essentially fixed: prudence, justice, fortitude, and moderation.

Philo, the Jewish philosopher of religion, and Clement of Alexandria tried to show that the Greek theory of the basic virtues is to be found in the Old Testament (Wisdom 8,7) . Ambrose was the first to say that the foundation of the cardinal virtues was Christ. Jerome, his contemporary, speaks of them as a team of four horses that bring Christ's charioteer directly to his goal. Augustine, Gregory the Great, John of Damascus, Alcuin, Rhabanus Maurus, Peter Lombard – those are the names of the most important bearers of tradition through whom the idea of presenting man's duty in a meaningful series of virtues was kept alive within the Christian doctrine about life. This idea was then, finally, made by Thomas Aquinas into a formal structural principle of a philosophical and theological doctrine of morality encompassing both the four cardinal virtues of prudence, justice, fortitude and moderation and the theological virtues of faith, hope, and love. Because of its differentiated and unified nature, this doctrine can be seen as classical. Thomas, using above all Aristotle as a basis, also presented the concept of "virtue" in all its elements and incorporated it into his theological anthropology.

A definition of virtue could look like this: virtue is an attitude by dint of which man is inclined to do what is good. But this does not give clear expression to the richness of what is really meant. The most important element is that virtue is a *habitus*. To give an adequate definition of the word *habitus* is difficult. What is meant is a particular way of being in yourself, of self-possession, through which a person really becomes certain of what he is. The concept *habitus* means something that lies between the *potentia* – the mere *possibility* of being and doing – and the *actus* – the *realization* of this possibility. The *habitus* is more than the mere possibility. It is a perfection of the *potentia*. But it is less than the realization of the possibility. It is a not yet perfect *actus*. *Habitus* means *potentia* in a leaning towards *actus*, possible being which is on the point of realization. *Habitus* is something distinctly human. It cannot be in God who is pure realization (*actus purus*), nor in natural things where the capacity to be and to act is realized of necessity. "Fire is true and right in its action – necessarily – but this is not the case for man when he does what is good" (Anselm of Canterbury). Because man is a being whose possibilities are not realized by natural necessity and are not already realized from the beginning, to do good he needs the *habitus*, by virtue of which he is imminently prepared to translate his capability into real action and being. Precisely this "being on the mark," ready to do what is good, is what is meant by the concept of virtue (as *habitus*); it is the extreme state of the capacity to be (*ultimum potentiae*). This announces a further element of the concept which emerges in the following clear formulation (by Thomas Aquinas): "Virtue is the force by which a being with the full strength of his own being (*potestas*) is able to follow his own drive for development (*impetus*)." One has to take this completely dynamic notion of world and man into account if one is not to misunderstand the ethics of Western Christianity. Man and world are not something static in the concrete world but have their *impetus*; they are caught up in a process of realization; they are moving, like a stone that has been thrown. Creation is something that is happening. But it is the perpetual, unceasing act of creation itself from which this dynamic originally derives its impetus and which still continues the process. But the goal of what is "happening" is called "realization." God created things "that they might be" (Wisdom 1,14). But the original impulse of the act of creation is so powerful that the creature cannot do otherwise – of himself, on the basis of his own innermost being – than likewise want to achieve this goal. This is his very nature – prior to all conscious intentions. The concept of virtue as carrying out the process already set in motion on the basis of creation includes the notion that the ethical as a whole can be characterized as secondary and subordinate. As norm for man's duty it is preceded by being as creation (the being of man and of his world). With regard to a logically formed concept of virtue, autonomistic idealism – with its now normal overestimation of ethics – is not acceptable, no more than is the notion that man, in making ethical decisions, is producing something totally new in itself. Long before there can be any question of a conscious decision of the will, the person, in making his decision, is already moving towards the good designed for him by nature. Long before the person can say a considered "yes" (or "no") the affirmation is already forming in him. And his decision is good insofar as it "follows" this affirmation which is already in train. The concept of virtue says that all that we can do is preceded by something we do *not* do – something we have received. This something which we have received in the being we are created with is not only prior to the deeds we perform on the basis of free choice, it is also to a large extent beyond the grasp of our intellect. This something we receive, which is prior to everything else, is not only beyond the range of our will, but also our reason is fundamentally unable to shed light on it. Only through acceptance and acknowledgement of this obscure and inalterable reality can moral action, as understood by the doctrine of virtue in the West, be at all meaningful. But, by linking man's real being together with his duty, his morality will retain a natural, relaxed quality: the good is what corresponds to the being both of man and of things. For this reason, the good, although it normally requires effort and self-control, is, when all is said and done, "natural" and "easy." This, too, is an essential element of the concept of virtue: virtue allows for the good being done *with joy.*

The real fruit and achievement of the thinking about man's morality – as incorporated in the Western doctrine of virtue – only becomes fully clear by contrast with its adversary, which is the idea not infrequently at work in the guise of an exclusively duty- and commandment-oriented ethic that thinks of what man "should do" in complete separation from what he "is." Out of this unrelated "other" world directives are given to a human being that is nothing and is worth nothing. These directives have nothing to do with the *being* of the person they address – the being which remains completely unimportant and irrelevant – but they are meant to be unconditionally binding on him. By contrast, the doctrine of the virtues does two things: first, the *being* of the moral person is explicitly focused on – both that which he has by nature, that comes with creation, and also his being right, the perfection of his being which he is meant to achieve by his own doing; second, the being of the moral person is not seen as mere "material" to become the object of an unrelated intervention by an arbitrary set of rules, but as an instance of admirable created reality that is required to flourish along the lines of development planned for it. In the doctrine of the virtues as developed in the tradition of Western thinking about human morality the very opposite of an enforced narrowness and suppression takes place; what happens, instead, is that a path opens, the coast is clear.

Hope – of What?
Easter 1957

The time that belongs most to us is the future. The past, even the moment that has just gone and which we call the "present," is part of our history, announcing and, of course, possibly thwarting what is "real" for us – what has still "not quite" become reality, but for the sake of which and towards which we really live. But memory, the dwelling in the faded glory of a past time, serves to keep us mindful of the dimensions of what could possibly be there again – a fulfillment that is yet to come. "It is strange how ready we are to be interrupted by something new, something unexpected. As if no point in our lives is so good that it could not be abandoned at any moment." "Ardent longing is the only genuine quality of all men . . . ."

"The hope principle"

This is the unusual title of the book in several volumes, from which the very true words above have been quoted. It is one of the strangest and most significant books to have been printed in Germany in recent years. Its author, who emerged a generation ago with his "Spirit of Utopia" (*Geist der Utopie*, 1923), is the Marxist theoretician Ernst Bloch, Professor at the university of Leipzig (recently gone into retirement). His aim is to show in an "Encyclopaedia of Hopes" that the home we have not yet managed to have is the basic theme of all real philosophy, which always – like a genuine work of art also – has "a utopian window" "with a landscape in the process of being formed." But the book is by no means limited to an overview of intellectual history. "What do we expect? What awaits us? . . . It depends on our learning to hope" – which is what we read on the very first page. Now, according to the author's opinion the hope to be learnt is none other than the *"docta spes,"* the hope as understood by dialectical materialism for a socialist change of the world."

What language tells us

At this point, of course, much as one earnestly tries ever again to respond to the realistic seriousness of this program – here again we encounter the fundamentally incorrect use of the word "hope" and therefore the questionable nature of the basic conception. Language resists the misuse of original words: one does not "hope for" something that can be produced by planning. Or does the use of the word reveal how much the ideological "praxis of concrete utopia" does in fact, in a hidden way, aim at something which is way beyond the bounds of human capabilities? In any case, wherever in the living spoken language there is talk of hope, there is always the connotation of something not in our power. If one says he hopes for favorable weather, health, the hand of divine providence, the flourishing of his children, the preservation of peace in the world, one knows that in all of these things there is an element that is not in his power. And yet nothing is so true as the fact that man is by his very nature a being that hopes. But one cannot agree with this idea without accepting that man is, by his very nature, looking forward to the fulfillment of hopes which he himself cannot bring about.

But this is not all that the wisdom intrinsic to

language is prepared to tell us. Its encoded message may not be readily formulatable by us, the daily speakers of this language, but we are fundamentally familiar with it. If, for example, we do not say of anyone he has lost all hope as long as he does not despair about ultimate success of his existence as a whole, then we know that precisely this success – and nothing else – is what is truly to be hoped for: the goal of his hope as such. Which means – and this is fully to be expected – that "the" hope can be accompanied by various kinds of despair, just as "the" main despair can be accompanied by various kinds of hope; that accordingly, in other words, the one with basic hope and the one who basically despairs are in no way easily distinguishable from one another. The ancients created a whole range of concepts and "tests" to use for uncovering a despair which was cleverly disguised by foreground forms of optimism.

"Theological" virtue

Everyone knows that ultimate "success" in life, success in one's existence as a whole, has always been referred to as "salvation" (Heil). It is the goal of "the" hope. But what does this salvation consist in? This question, as is clear from the outset, can only be discussed meaningfully if one is prepared to bring the ultimate opinions into play. Anyone who wants to avoid this has already decided to give up speaking seriously about the object of man's hope.

The great teachers of the Christian West have, without deviating, called hope a "theological virtue." There is something deeply disturbing in this, something which cannot easily be settled. Which means: there is, it is true, nothing at all to be said against the right to hope for things in this world, yet the fact that a person may have hopes of flourishing in natural things is not enough for him to be "in order" – even if these hopes concern something as significant as world peace and justice for all peoples of the world; it means that only the hope of divine salvation, eternal life, makes a person inwardly right. (This is precisely what is meant by the concept of virtue: being right in oneself, correct.) We must be aware of the direction this thesis is taking. It is aimed not just against a purely innerworldly activism which maintains that there is no hope left once we can do nothing more, but also against the pure otherworldly view of a supernaturalism outside of history, which, in a defeatist attitude, despairs of the world of human politics. The unsettling element introduced by the thesis that hope has a "theological" character still has an impact on the present opposition between Christianity and Marxism. But the most disturbing aspect is the decisiveness with which the insight – already sensed by Plato – is realized: that the "greatest hope" can only be fulfilled through initiation into the mysteries.

In this context the other more important question can be answered: not "hope – for what?," but "hope – on the basis of what?" Christendom's sacred book has given the answer in the form of a negation: "The" (main) hope means nothing "if Christ is not risen."

The Hidden Nature of Hope and Despair
A contribution to discussion

There is a form of despair which is not easily seen as despair. And there is a form of hope which, to the superficial gaze, can really look like despair, although it is hope of the most triumphal kind. This is what I mean by the "hidden nature" both of hope and despair. I am not saying that every hope and every despair is necessarily and always hidden. I am only saying that both hope and despair can appear in a form which is at first not distinguishable. And this is what is to be discussed here.

I feel it is not unimportant to speak about this. The theme "hope" has taken on a direct significance for life in our present age, which in a special sense seems exposed to the temptation to despair. It must be all the more relevant to penetrate the mask of misleading appearances and to identify behind the – at first – indistinguishable forms the true face of real hope and real despair.

I am in no way concerned with presenting a series of more or less original ideas about a somewhat marginal theme. I would like to try, with reference to this one specific point, the relationship which links the teachings of the ancients about hope and despair with the reality of the present human situation; for it is the ancients, the great teachers of the West, who speak of the hidden nature both of hope and despair. My essay is aimed at making visible a little of the light that falls from that "ancient truth" onto the reality that we ourselves are.

* * *

Søren Kierkegaard called the hidden form of despair

"despair from weakness." This despair, he says, consists in man not daring to be himself, even explicitly not wanting to be himself. He refuses to be what he really is; he does not accept his own being.

With this concept "despair from weakness" Kierkegaard has, consciously or otherwise, taken up an age-old notion that was current in Western teaching about life: namely, the idea of that particular kind of "sloth" which usually appears amongst the seven deadly sins (*vitia capitalia*) as *acedia*. In the current popular mind, the original idea of sloth (laziness) as being one of the seven deadly sins has been reversed to mean almost the opposite. "Sloth," in the thinking of the average man, appears as belonging to the middle-class world of commerce – meaning: lack of diligence; laziness; lack of the desire to work. But when the great teachers of West Christendom called "sloth of the heart" a sin they were not endorsing the capitalist regime of unceasing labour. What they meant by *acedia* is that a person does not engage with working at his own self-realization, that he refuses to make the required contribution to his own truly human existence. This in no way refers to any external action but to the carrying out of his own personal being, a duty which we know – without a word being spoken, yet unmistakably – that we are required to perform. Not to respond to this demand, to answer with "no": that would be the essence of "sloth," *acedia*. In sloth, which is a sin, man resists the demand which comes with the dignity of his own status; he refuses to be the spiritual being endowed with the capacity to decide; above all, he does not want to be that to which God has raised him – a level of being far above what his purely human nature can achieve. In a word, the person does not want to be something which, however, he cannot cease to be: a spiritual person who cannot be satisfied with anything less than God himself. The person is a "son of God," rightful heir to eternal life.

The ancients also saw sloth in connection with despair. They refer to *acedia* as a form of depression, that paralyzing *tristitia saeculi*, namely, of which Paul said that it brings about death. But not only that. The ancients also say expressly that this sad sloth is already the beginning of despair – just as Kierkegaard sees "despair from weakness" as the preliminary stage of real and complete despair, the reflected "despair of self-affirmation."

Well, that may be all very interesting. But where is the special relevance for modern-day man? And besides, where is a "hidden nature" and a "deceptive appearance" which need, with all due care, to be uncovered and unmasked? I shall try to supply an answer. It has already been said that in the ancient doctrine about life, sloth – *acedia* – is considered one of the (seven) deadly sins. The *vitia capitalia* are wrongdoings from which other wrongdoings proceed – so to speak, naturally – as from a "source." *Caput* means "source." It makes sense, and is necessary, to speak not just about the source itself but about the "river area" which is supplied by it. If one looks back from the mouth of the river, so to speak, to the source – the sin of sloth – suddenly the link with the form of existence of contemporary man emerges with intense clarity. It is then quite impossible not to notice it.

From not wanting to be oneself, from the refusal to carry through one's own being, from the innermost conflict of the person with himself – in a word, from sloth – springs, amongst other things, according to the ancients, the "wandering unrest of the spirit." Whoever, in the deepest region of his soul, is not one with himself, whoever does not want to be what he, however, fundamentally is – such a person cannot live with himself, cannot be at home with himself. He has to make the (of course) vain attempt to break out of his own center – for example, into restless work for the sake of work or also into the unquenchable curiosity for pure spectacle, which is, in truth, not a quest for knowledge but only for "possibilities of abandoning oneself to the world" (Heidegger), i.e. for possibilities of avoiding oneself.

The ancient doctrine about *acedia* is, indeed, far richer. It speaks, for example, of the unrest that drives a person from one part of the world to another; it speaks also of *verbositas*, the endless talk that fills up everyday existence. But I suggest that we focus on *these* two phenomena, and these alone: the lack of leisure in the world of work, and the curiosity for pure spectacle. Both occur in our world with a claim that affects the whole of life. That this is true of the absolutizing of work hardly needs further discussion. Our world is a world of work run along totalitarian lines. But also the fact that the real world of things and the true life of man threatens to be smothered by an artificial world of empty, stimulating things which only serve to feed our curiosity for spectacle – this, too, can hardly be challenged. Where can a sphere of life be found which does not allow access to the instruments that generate public curiosity?

A further consideration is that both phenomena – the programmatic absolutizing of the ideal of work and the degenerate curiosity for spectacle – are surrounded by an enormous amount of forced optimism, radiating confidence about life, and loud proclamations about progressiveness. Everyone knows that, in the world of work described, belief in progress has been declared a social obligation. And it is likewise known that "keep smiling" and "happy ending" have, from the beginning, belonged to the main elements of the artificial world in which curiosity for spectacle has found a replacement for "the fullness of life."

And yet these forms of optimism are of no ultimate significance vis-à-vis the despair which is their origin – even if this origin remains shut up in the innermost recesses of ourselves so that no sound of pain is heard outside of it, perhaps not even in our own consciousness.

We can perhaps say that such hidden despair is the natural companion of secularization. Secularization is by no means regression into heathenism. Heathenism looks to the future, to the *adventus*; but secularized man, having no future and full of despair, wants to undo the *adventus* – that has already taken place – and his own elevation that came with the *adventus*; for he wishes that God had not given him this gift but had "left him in peace."

It does not have to be said that all goals aimed at purely in this world – whether a classless society, a five-year plan, prosperity, survival after a fashion, or, even more vulgarly: "enjoy the day" (because tomorrow we are dead) – insofar as they are understood as ultimate goals have one thing in common: they don't dare to face up to the greatness of the human person. Despite the resounding and sonorous tones of optimism with which they are usually proclaimed, they are usually forms of despair – that despair from weakness, which means that the person does not want to be what he, however, is and remains to be, and that he does not want to attain the end which is really designed for him and is appropriate to him.

* * *

There is also a hidden form of hope. This is now to be discussed.

Hope always says: it will turn out well; it will be good in the end – this applies to creation as a whole, to man, to myself. The Christian's hope means nothing different from this. The good end for the Christian's hope has the names: eternal life, salvation, bliss, a New Heaven and a New Earth.

But the Christian's hope cannot be separated from particular ideas about the structure of the historical world. And this is the reason why this hope, in the most extreme case, can seem to be hidden, so that to the eye of the non-Christian it must be almost unrecognizable and seem very like despair. That notion of the historical world, i.e. of the world of human beings, has the connotation that in it evil possesses power, or even that evil, as a force belonging to this world, can appear as the dominant force. – The virtue of fortitude, for example, has long been understood, according to Augustine, as an irrefutable witness to the existence and power of evil in the world. But, above all, according to the classical doctrine about fortitude, the real act of the brave man is not attack but standing firm. The reason for this is not that action is valued less than suffering. The reason is that the real test of bravery only begins when the person is handed over, defenseless, to the superior power of evil. This explains something which is not at all self-evident: that for the Christian understanding of existence the highest incarnation of bravery is not the armed hero bursting with strength but the martyr, and that the most extreme act of bravery is witness in one's own blood.

Here a further word must be said about the idea of the end of human history as it is conceived of in the history of human thought – from John on Patmos down to Wladimir Solowjew. According to this notion, to put it succinctly, history will finish with an historical catastrophe – and, indeed, one brought about within the historical process itself. Human history will not "cease" simply on the basis of an external fact in the way that the song of a bird is silenced by a shot from a boy's gun. No, the song will be sung to the end, but, considered within our history, it will be a dissonance. Undoubtedly, this idea that the final catastrophe has an historical character, that it will result from the free action of men, has, for anyone who reflects on our history, something far more terrifying and unsettling than the notion of an exclusively cosmic catastrophe – for instance, the destruction of the planet "Earth" by an external force. For it means, as well, that human history *always*, and therefore also *today*, is heading for this catastrophic end. The dissonance of the final catastrophe is more or less clearly audible. I don't believe that we can dispense ourselves from this thought.

The dreadful nature of this thought is only seen in its entirety when we think of the name used in tradition to signify the final catastrophic situation in our history. This name is the "rule of the Antichrist." It does not merely refer to the abstract rejection of Christ on principle. But it describes how the Antichrist is to be thought of as a powerful figure of this world. Just as on the basis of his *potentia saecularis* (as Thomas says) he is to be seen as an eminently historical and political figure, and in no way as a heretic who is interesting only in the context of "church history" and of whom the rest of the world needs to take no notice, so, too – and this is what Western thinking about history tells us – the fight against Christ right across the whole world will take on the form of a political battle for power against the Church, against Christendom, yes, again as Thomas says, against all "good men." But the word "battle" is an inaccurate expression. We are not dealing with two partners who are looking for a mode of coexistence. The world state of the Antichrist will not in the real sense undertake a battle against the Church but will "persecute" her. But persecution means a fight by the powerful against those who have no power. Here again, for the Christian and for the Church the only form of resistance remaining to them will be the defenseless standing firm, the most extreme form of which is witness in blood.

The figure of this witness, the martyr, emerges, therefore, as the most extreme answer that the Christian doctrine has for us about the nature of the historical world. It is the figure of a man for whom, in the eyes of the world, there is no more hope, who is delivered over, defenseless, to the superior force of evil. Every form of optimism in this life has then become meaningless and the hands of the natural campaigner are literally bound. Yet the martyr is unthinkable without a downright triumphal strength based on his hope. This hope is, of course, the one of which I said it is so hidden that it is almost unrecognizable – not just for the man of this world and for the non-Christian, but even for the average Christian himself.

Precisely here we are forced to see what Christian hope really consists of. We have no other recourse but to realize this Christian hope within ourselves – provided we want to continue existing alertly and without despairing. This is the painful benefit arising from completely catastrophic times and therefore also from the present era: that we are prevented from overlooking the apocalyptic dimension of history; that we are forced "to know our situation in the world" (Donoso Cortés).

The question, therefore, that we are compelled to consider concerns the hope of the person who is preparing for bearing witness in blood. This person is not really the exceptional individual. Strictly speaking, the martyr is not the exception. We say it with a shudder that the willingness to accept martyrdom – as all teachers in Christendom tell us – is one of the fundamental aspects of Christian existence. This means that the existence of *every* Christian is accompanied by the inner possibility of such witness. The world behind the Iron Curtain is just one great example – of which we are daily reminded. There is no more radical way of posing the question about the essence of Christian hope than to ask about the nature of the martyr's hope. There is no one in the world able to know more deeply what hope is – not merely to say and to think one has hope, but really to hope – no one can know it the way the person does who, in the most extreme circumstances, is called on to practice the virtue of fortitude, the virtue of endurance. Of course, those with this knowledge have either fallen silent in death or they keep silence. However, the martyrs' knowledge has been taken up into the treasury of Christian wisdom handed down to us. Even if we are not able to speak about it without a feeling of shame, we are not allowed to suppress this knowledge and ignore it.

Precisely in the hidden nature of the martyr's hope

we see a fundamental aspect of all truly Christian hope: namely, that hope is a *theological virtue*. There is, of course, such a thing as natural hope. But this natural hope is not a virtue just because it is hope. Natural hope does not necessarily make a person inwardly right. More concretely: a person does not have this inner rightness by the mere fact of hoping for a happy old age or the flourishing of his children or peace in the world or that humanity might be spared the fate of self-destruction. There is nothing at all to be said against any of these hopes, and we would consider a person lucky if he can unreservedly entertain such hopes. But who would want to say that they are intrinsic to the inner rightness of man, that they are quite simply a "virtue"? The situation in the case of justice is quite different. The justice even of natural man is a virtue by the very fact of being justice. But hope becomes a virtue only as *theological* hope, i.e. as hope for a salvation that cannot be had in the natural world.

And yet Christian hope does not lose sight of our historical, created world. This, too, can be seen from consideration of the Christian martyr, who is something incomparable. It is not enough to consider him as one who dies for his convictions – as if the truth content of his convictions were of no relevance. What distinguishes the Christian martyr and makes him incomparable is that, despite all the awful things that happen to him, he "says not one word against God's creation" (E. Peterson). The distinguishing element is that the Christian martyr, despite everything, does not revile natural reality, but, on the contrary, still finds creation "very good."

Thus the hope of the martyr combines three elements: the real object of hope is eternal life and not some kind of well-being that can be found in the world – that is the first element. The second element is the active affirmation of the created world in every sphere. The third element is readiness for a catastrophic end caused by forces within our history.

The combination of these three elements – how could it be otherwise? – is full of dynamic tensions. And it is not easy to endure these tensions and to live them out. That means that the Christian's hope is naturally, and continually, exposed to the temptation to escape into a supernaturalism that ignores history, or into a purely innerworldly activism, or into a tragic and defeatist stance that is repugnant to creation. Whenever we care to take stock we are continually confronted with these back-to-front ideas of Christian hope.

Naturally, these reversals do not have their real basis in any theoretical problem. The person who is challenged by the need to accept the apocalyptic dimension of our history is not primarily the thinker but the person who lives a directly spiritual existence.

There is very little sense, therefore, in wanting to interpret and justify the painful silence of the martyr by rational argumentation: his hope does not emerge from its hidden state in this way. More – and something other – is required than pure reflection and mental exertion if we are to succeed in becoming aware of the hidden reality. This applies to the reality of the hidden despair of the innerworldly person as well as to the triumphal reality of the hidden hope of the martyr.

Concluding note

The above thoughts were presented in a lecture held at the "Fourth International Congress for Peace and

Christian Culture" in Florence (19-25 June, 1955) which was arranged by its initiator, the Lord Mayor of Florence Professor Giorgio La Pira, with the overall theme "Human Hope and Theological Hope."

The designation "contribution to discussion" defines the limits set to the claims of this speech: it is expressly *not* an attempt to give a comprehensive and well-rounded account of the relationship between natural and supernatural hope, but rather to formulate a quite specific aspect which – as could certainly be suspected from the outset – might receive too little attention at the Congress.

In the discussion in which Père Jean Daniélou and Professor Marcel Reding were the main participants, several objections were raised. The first was that the Christian is obliged, by love, to share the earthly hopes of the poor and to work towards their realization, whereas the accentuation of the eschatological aspect could all too easily serve as an alibi for the lack of practical love (Daniélou). The second was that, in purely general terms, man's natural hopes were not sufficiently valued in Thomistic/Aristotelian ethics (Reding).

In my reply I made the following points: first, we must contribute whatever we can to the realization of man's hopes on earth, but we should not believe that there is no hope left when there is nothing more we can do. Second, the temptation of defeatist quietism is always present, as is the temptation of supernaturalism that ignores history. But purely innerworldly activism is also a degenerate form of Christian hope. There is no ultimately effective recipe for excluding these dangers from the outset. What is required is continual vigilance *in all three* directions.

Third, not one word can be said against man's right to his natural hopes nor against any form of optimism in life. But the question here is whether such hopes *eo ipso* make man "right in himself," i.e. whether such hope can simply be called "virtue." To answer in the negative and to say that hope is a virtue only when it is a theological virtue does not seem to me to be "Thomistic" but simply "Christian."

Fourth, although readiness for a catastrophic end caused by forces within our history is a necessary part of Christian hope, it is, however, not good to speak much about it. Perhaps one should, with a kind of "arcane discipline," be silent about it – and work actively in this human world. But being silent is not the same as suppressing and denying its existence.

The Seed Requires Soil

The complaint that the Germans are still not prepared to "accept" the act of 20 July 1944 and to see it as concerning them and that, despite all the occasional praise given them, the men of this day have not been given their due status and place in the consciousness of the people – this complaint, which keeps on cropping up, seems to be justified. The fact itself cannot be argued away. But the question about the why and the wherefore is not easy to answer. When you think about it you see yourself confronted with a much more far-reaching phenomenon: it seems that the victims of the reign of violence have – in a frightening way – largely been forgotten. And this before their death has been lamented and officially mourned by the people. The convulsive isolated acts and also the almost complete lack of resonance achieved by individual attempts, so to speak, to force remembrance by the erection of warning memorials are only a few of the signs amongst many.

The endeavor to find an explanation, when faced with the immediacy of political mistakes and resentment, might produce something psychologically plausible. But, on the whole, that will hardly get to the heart of the matter. We have to suspect the presence of a more deeply rooted disorder, for it goes without saying that something is not in order. And of course it seems that the problem is of such a kind that it cannot be removed by a simple decision, and certainly not by a public campaign. Perhaps – and this is a serious question to ask – perhaps we have forgotten what, in truth, we as a people live from and from what sources the *bonum commune* is nourished, that seemingly indestructible "good" of our shared existence that cannot be completely extinguished even by tyranny.

Perhaps we have lost the clear insight that it is not just the obvious harvest of scientific and technological or even of "cultural" achievement that realizes the common good of a nation; that for this, on the contrary, contributions of an *obscure* origin are needed – even in normal times where law is functioning properly – contributions to the *bonum commune* which, by their very nature, are hardly noticeable let alone subject to control. Who would want to say, for example, in what way the achievement – which cannot be doubted – comes about, by which truth remains present in a people? The ancients have attributed this achievement to those who live for contemplation, for which reason it is necessary "for the perfection of human society" that these silent and hidden people exist. Contributions of this kind are naturally, by their very nature, in danger of being forgotten and declared non-existent.

Furthermore, there is a still more hidden living root of the *bonum commune: sacrifice.* It is more hidden because the person sacrificing himself falls silent at the very moment of sacrifice. And if modern violent tyrannies have an understanding of anything it is how to deprive the silence of the victim of any possibility of making a statement and to make his silence complete – so complete, that it is difficult to notice that anything is missing.

It is clear that sacrifice is understood here in a highly active sense. Language usage that speaks, without differentiation, of the victims – sacrifices – of the war is very inexact, which can be seen by the fact that it, as we know, would have to use the same term for the executioners of the men of 20 July as for the men themselves. Of course, we are speaking here not of the details of what these men planned and carried out. We are speaking of what, by their actions, they took upon themselves. We are speaking of their sacrifice – and of the fact that the true life of a people is nourished by such acts of sacrifice.

In them alone, when injustice rules, is justice not forgotten. In their sacrifice, this true elite grasps and exercises the office of the true ruler which has been betrayed by those in fact in power: namely, to look after justice.

To say it again: have we forgotten that we need such invisible foundations if the life of a people is to be healthy or at least capable of healing?

"The degree of danger and willingness for sacrifice demanded of us today presupposes more than good ethical principles." With this sentence, the young Helmuth James Count von Moltke, executed in January 1945 – one of the most spiritual figures in the German resistance – explicitly revokes the opinion he had held earlier that "faith in God is not essential." – This gives rise to another question which is worth considering: to be aware of and to acknowledge the fruitfulness of sacrifice, is the same kind of faith presupposed as that which is required for the act of sacrifice itself?

While the effect of the sacrifice is by no means limited to the psychological sphere, neither are we here dealing with some form of magical automatism. To put it differently: the fruit of the sacrifice can also be wasted. The saying about the blood of the martyrs sowing seeds does express an unquestionable truth, but it includes the condition that the martyr not be left alone and forgotten, but that the seed be sown in the soil of memory and veneration.

Religion and Freedom

It is an indisputable fact that "religion" – more precisely, the churches and also individual personalities shaped by their religious convictions – offered resistance to tyranny, whether in the form of National Socialism or Bolshevism, and stood up for freedom, religious and otherwise. But I still do not believe that the opposition between, on the one hand, a consistently secular rationalism and liberalism and, on the other hand, religion, is based on a misunderstanding that the present experience renders meaningless. In the "Provisional Program" of the Congress for Cultural Freedom (Berlin 1960) there was a formulation which suggested such an interpretation: "In the eighteenth century religion was understood as the main enemy of freedom but proved to be a citadel of opposition to the tyranny of the third Reich." This "but" is an expression of surprise, but to me it seems that in this there is nothing surprising. One could even say, with a slight exaggeration, that, for the same reason that religion in the eighteenth century was held to be an enemy of freedom and is today held to be an enemy of rationalistic liberalism, the church (and the type of individual personalities mentioned) offered resistance to the tyrannical regimes. This shows how complicated the problem is when we tackle the question of whether religion impedes or favors the realization of freedom.

It is correct that both liberalism and Christianity have fought for freedom. But it should not be forgotten that this battle is characterized by reasons and aims which are very different in either case. I would like to make some comments about these differences.

In a lecture at the Congress just mentioned, Count

Helmuth von Moltke was rightly referred to as a Christian freedom fighter. But I cannot recall ever having read in his letters anything that suggests that this noble man, who consciously lived the life of a Christian, offered resistance for the sake of the "idea of freedom" and fought and died for "freedom." The same can be said of many others who, out of religious conviction, rose up against tyranny. The official Church announcements also do not speak explicitly of freedom. Instead they speak of truth, of justice, of injustice, of the dignity of the human person and of its being disregarded, of the right of parents to educate their children the way they see fit – and so on. Naturally, freedom is also demanded. And naturally freedom is also for the Christian a fundamental, indispensable and indisputable value. Even if no end of discussion can remove from the history of Christendom such shameful and awful things like the Inquisition, it cannot be denied that they happened *in contradiction to* Christian "theory" itself, while the acts of violence of the totalitarian regimes – whether National Socialist or Bolshevist – are strictly in accordance with their own principles. Only the example of Stalin's definition needs to be cited, according to which the dictatorship of the proletariat is the rule of the proletariat over the bourgeoisie, without any restriction by law and basing itself on force. Thomas Aquinas, on the other hand, a contemporary of the Inquisition, said such extreme things as: for a person who thinks it is wrong to believe in Christ it is *not permissible* to believe in him, and it is better for him to die excommunicated than to act against his conscience. However, "the idea of freedom" plays, in the context of Christian teaching, a fundamentally different role than it plays in the context of the rationalistic and liberalist view of the world. I don't think a liberal will say that there can be too much freedom; he may not even admit that there is such a thing as abuse of freedom. The Christian, on the other hand, is very definitely of this opinion. It is true that there can never be too much justice, and to speak of an abuse of justice would be nonsense. But it is quite possible to abuse freedom.

Another distinction between the Christian and the liberalist notion of freedom seems to me even more important. To understand it one must consider that the "idea" of freedom is *one* thing and the "reality" of freedom is *another*. One thing peculiar to the Christian notion of freedom, it seems to me, is the conviction that in this world of human history certain things only have reality by *not* being deliberately (as "idea") focused on and proclaimed. Clearly there are good things which we do not gain when we consciously or even exclusively strive for them. They are given as something extra when we are expressly striving for something else. This is a conceptual structure which also has validity elsewhere. For example, according to one of the results of depth psychology, nothing impedes the realization of psychological health more than the express or even exclusive will to be healthy and to remain so; thus health as an explicitly proclaimed "idea" stands in the way of the "reality" of health. – This has certain implications for the theme "freedom." It was said in the general program of that Congress: "not all ideas promote freedom" and we are called upon to "examine all ideas to see what guarantees or dangers they present for freedom." One could venture to say that amongst the ideas that stand in the way of achieving freedom the very idea of freedom itself is to be found. That is, of course, a somewhat exaggerated formulation which can easily be misunderstood and misinterpreted. But I think it is right to this extent: whoever fights for freedom must above all fight for values with a particular *content* (truth, justice, human dignity, etc.). And this is exactly what characterizes the Christian and religious resistance against tyranny. This is known to us from its documents.

I believe we should not underestimate the part played by such goals – defined by content – in the struggle for freedom in the Polish "October" and the Hungarian uprising. Paul Ignotus, President of the Hungarian Writers in Exile, said at the Congress that for the Hungarian resistance fighters the "traditional" values were the decisive ones. In Hungary, "traditional" as good as means "Christian." And Herbert Lüthy contradicted the opinion that in Poland and Hungary it was a question of nationalism; on the contrary, it was a question of the right social form; but that, too, is clearly an idea with definite content.

It is very difficult, and for the modern consciousness it is *the* difficult task, to give the justification of such values and goals with value content, the express affirmation of which is the true and perhaps the only necessary presupposition for the realization of freedom. In the theory of the tyrannies, for example, the rights of the person – based on human nature – are denied; this is precisely what lies at the foundation of the lack of freedom. I believe that, in the field of intellectual debate, the problem cannot be dealt with unless this foundation is destroyed, i.e., by achieving the insight, first, that there *is* such a thing as human nature (which Sartre's brand of existentialism is known to contest); and second, insight about the way in which, and on the basis of which, this human nature and, consequently, every human individual, has inalienable rights which every partner must recognize. Whoever has no answer to this has, one may fear, little hope of justifying the demand for freedom.

In the discussion there were repeated complaints (made by Salvador de Madariaga and Theodor Litt) that the "West," and, above all, young students, had no clear idea about freedom. I wonder whether this frightening phenomenon is not explained partly by the fact that the youth have not come to any clear conviction about the binding nature of these content values, on which alone the formal idea of freedom can be based.

What religion has contributed to the realization of freedom seems to me, in summary, the following: first, the simple naming of those content values, the realization of which brings freedom as an extra; second, the justification and sanctioning of these same values, the binding force of which has its source beyond human norms.

Leisure and Human Existence

Whoever speaks of leisure these days immediately finds himself on the defensive. He faces opposition from a force which at first seems to be the stronger. The situation is not made simpler by the opposition being "someone else"; instead, it is an inner debate. And, still worse, if we are caught unawares and asked what it is we are defending, we are not able to give a very exact answer. When, for example, *Aristotle* says: "We work in order to have leisure" we must be honest and admit that we don't know what this offensive sentence means.

This, then, is the way things stand.

Accordingly, the first question is: what is meant by leisure? What does this concept mean within the great tradition?

It seems to me fitting to attempt an answer by first speaking of the contrary – what we know as "overvaluation of work." This is, of course, a rather provisional term, for "work" can mean at least three things. Work can be taken to mean "activity as such." It can also mean effort, strain, drudgery. A third meaning is found in common parlance, according to which work means useful activity, above all, socially useful activity. Which of these three concepts is meant when we speak of the "overvaluation of work"? I would say that all three are meant! There is an overvaluation of activity as well as an overvaluation of effort and the difficult; and, last but not least, there is an overvaluation of social function. Precisely this is the three-faced demon that has to be dealt with by anyone who undertakes the defense of leisure.

140

Overvaluation of activity as such. – By this I mean the inability simply to let something happen; the inability to receive, to be on the receiving end. It is the "unconditional activity" of which Goethe said that it brings about bankruptcy. The most extreme formulation in which this heresy has appeared until now I find in a sentence of *Hitler's*: "Every activity is meaningful, even a criminal act; all passivity, on the other hand, is meaningless." Naturally, this is a crazy formulation; it is quite simply absurd. But "milder" forms of this madness are, in general, characteristic of the present world.

Overvaluation of effort and difficulty. – This, too, exists, even if seldom. One can even say that the average ethical attitude of the "decent" modern person is based to a large extent on this overvaluation of difficulty: the good is by its very nature difficult; and anything that does not require effort has no ethical value. *Schiller* treated this thesis ironically in a verse aimed at *Kant*: "I am happy to be of service to friends, but, sadly, I am that way inclined/Therefore often I worry that I am not virtuous therein." The "ancients" – by which I mean the great Greeks *Plato* and *Aristotle*, but also the teachers of Western Christendom – did not believe that the good is by virtue of its nature, and therefore always and necessarily, difficult. They knew that precisely the highest forms of realization of the good are always effortless, because by their very nature they proceed from love. And also the highest forms of knowing – (for example, the flash of inspiration, genuine contemplation) are not "intellectual work," they, too, are effortless – because by their very nature they are a gift. "Gift" – this is perhaps a key word. If we think of the strange preference for the difficult ingrained in the face of contemporary man,

141

characterizing him as prepared for pain (it is far more characteristic, I think, than the much criticized "craving for pleasure"!) – if we think of this we are suddenly faced with the question: is not the most fundamental reason for this the refusal to accept anything from anyone, no matter from whom?

Overvaluation of social function. – Little needs to be said to show that this is a dominant characteristic of contemporary society. We should not think that this applies only to the totalitarian Five Year Plans, where what is really bad is not the planning but the claim that here, exclusively, is the measure of value for life as a whole – not only for industrial production but equally for the organizing of individual free time. The dictatorship of pure utility can also have a strong influence in the non-totalitarian world. – At this point an old distinction should be called to mind, namely, the distinction between the "artes liberales" and the "artes serviles," between "free" and "servile" activities. This distinction means that there are, on the one hand, human activities which have their meaning within themselves, and, on the other hand, there are those which serve a purpose outside of themselves, i.e. they are merely useful. At first sight, this seems to be a rather old-fashioned and pedantic idea. But in fact it is a question of something quite politically relevant. If we translate the question "Are there free activities" into the jargon of the totalitarian world of work, this is the result: is there human activity which, by its very nature, does not require to be (and cannot be) justified by applying the criterion of a Five Year Plan? The ancients have answered this question very decisively in the affirmative. The answer from the totalitarian world of work is equally uncompromising: no, man is in every respect a functionary; "free" activity that does not serve social needs is undesirable and therefore to be "liquidated."

If now, with this three-faced overvaluation in mind, we turn our gaze to the concept of "leisure," it becomes immediately clear that there is no room for it in this world of work. Not only does it make no sense, but it is also morally suspect. – And, indeed, there is here an absolute incompatibility. The idea of leisure is diametrically opposed to the totalitarian idea of the "worker," and this applies to each of the three aspects of which I have spoken.

Against the absolutization of activity. – Leisure is precisely "non-activity"; it is a form of silence. Leisure is precisely that form of silence which is a presupposition for hearing something. Only the silent person is able to hear. Leisure is the attitude of purely receptive immersion of the self into reality; the soul's openness, to which alone are given the very great fulfilling insights that no "intellectual work" can achieve.

Against the overvaluing of effort. Leisure is an attitude of celebration. And celebration means the opposite of effort. Whoever fundamentally mistrusts ease is, by the same token, both incapable of leisure and of celebrating a feast. Of course, for a feast something else is also needed – which we will now deal with.

Against the overvaluation of social function. Leisure means precisely that one is removed from social function. But leisure is not to be confused with taking a pause. A pause, whether it lasts an hour or three weeks, means recovery from work for the sake of work. Leisure is something quite different. The meaning of leisure is not that man functions without disturbance but that in the middle of performing his social function he remains human, i.e. that he remains capable of looking beyond the narrowly defined milieu where he functions, to see the world as a whole and to celebrate it – to see himself as someone related to the totality of the world through a free activity, i.e. one which has meaning of itself and is not "engaged."

True culture does not flourish except in the soil of leisure. Here we mean by "culture" all that goes beyond the basic needs of life but is nevertheless indispensable for a full human existence. But if culture lives from leisure, what does leisure live from? How can man be put in a position where he can "achieve leisure" (as the Greeks said)? What can be done to prevent his becoming nothing but a "worker" who is completely identified with a function?

I confess that I am unable to answer these questions with concrete and practicable instructions. The real difficulty is of such a kind that it cannot be solved by a mere decision of the will, no matter how well intended. Still, it is possible to show why this is so. – We know that doctors have been indicating for some time now how important leisure is for health – and they are undoubtedly correct in this. But one cannot bring about leisure in order to remain healthy or to become healthy – not even "to rescue culture"! There are things we do when we consider them meaningful in themselves. It is not possible to do them "so that" something else happens (we cannot, for example, love a person "so that . . ." and "in order to . . ."). Certain priorities cannot be reversed. To attempt to reverse them is not only not appropriate, but it quite simply does not work.

For our question, this means the following: if leisure

is not experienced as something meaningful in itself then it is simply impossible to achieve it. Here we need to speak again about feasts. A feast combines all three elements which make up the concept of leisure: first, non-activity and rest; second, ease; third, separation from the usual daily work function. Everyone knows what a problematic thing it is for people these days to celebrate a feast. The reason why feasts fail is the same as the reason why leisure fails.

At this point a thought inevitably occurs which, as I have frequently experienced, is very unwelcome to most people: to celebrate a feast means to express affirmation of the world as a whole in a manner different from the everyday. Whoever does not consider the world to be "good" and "in order" cannot celebrate a feast any more than he can "achieve leisure." This means that leisure is tied to the presupposition that the person affirms the world as well as his own nature. And now comes the idea that is equally unpopular and unavoidable: the most extreme form of affirmation of the world is praise of God, praise of the Creator – religious service. This, then, also identifies the ultimate root of leisure.

We must prepare ourselves for the likelihood that enormous efforts will be made to avoid the consequences of this insight – for example, through the attempt to introduce artificial holidays, which would mean avoiding the ultimate and true affirmation of the world. This would happen through the politically backed immense financial outlay for external arrangements to produce the appearance of genuine celebration. In reality, this organizing of "free time" through pseudo festivals is just another, more breathless, form of work.

It would be a misunderstanding to think that this

thesis about the fundamental cultic character of all celebration and about the cultic origin of leisure is specifically Christian. Perhaps what is today usually referred to as
"secularism" is not so much dechristianization as the loss
of some fundamental insights which belong to the corpus
of natural human wisdom handed down to us. The thesis about leisure and cult seems to me to belong to this
corpus. It is, for example, the pre-Christian Greek Plato,
who, as an old man, formulated it in a magnificent mythical image. Plato poses the question whether there is no
breathing space for human beings, who are evidently
born for work and hardship. He answers: yes, there is a
breathing space: "The gods, taking pity on the human
race born to hardship, have given them as breathing
space the recurring cultic holidays and, as festival companions, the muses and their leaders Apollo and
Dionysus – so that, nourishing themselves in the festive
company of the gods, they could stand upright and
straight." And the other great Greek, Aristotle, "more
critical than his teacher, Plato," and, as we know, not
inclined to speak in mythical images – even Aristotle also
formulated the same insight, in his more sober way. In
the *Nicomachean Ethics*, where the sentence already cited
is to be found (we work in order to have leisure) – in this
same book we read that to lead the life of leisure is not
possible for man as man but only insofar as something
divine lives in him.

The Necessary but Also Impossible
Business of Teaching
A Speech Made at the Inauguration
of a Pedagogical Academy (1958)

If it is true that education (understood as being cultured, the fruit, therefore, that results from human educative activity taking place in proper, favorable circumstances) also requires that we reflect on such questions that are at the very root of our own profession, on such an occasion as today's, the guest feels called on – and in my case the well-wisher and guest is not someone from outside, not just a visitor and observer but someone who completely belongs and is in every conceivable way involved – if the *fruit* of education is that the person knows how things really are in the world as a whole, that he knows it not only with the head but also with the heart; and if, accordingly, education as the *activity* of educating means presenting the whole of reality to the gaze of the student and listener, giving access to the totality of the world and showing the multiplicity of what we encounter to be both one and a whole; if all this is the case, it is only to be expected that anyone engaged in education in our era will be completely baffled and startled by the obvious impossibility of meeting the demands which are made of this activity and to which it is exposed. Are we not dealing with a task which is, from the very beginning, impossible? How can I bring anything to anyone's gaze if I don't see it myself? And how can I teach something which I don't know myself? Of course, one should not exaggerate. Our knowledge and our skill is not to be denied. With regard to the real world we are not, after all, inexperienced and naïve. And who would want to deny that it is worthwhile, meaningful, important – and even necessary – to hand on to a young generation such exact, reliable knowledge and the control over the world it enables? However, here we need to insert a cautionary and definite "but." It is not such exact knowledge (about the structure of matter, the structure of cells, about the behavioral patterns of plants and animals, about the history and forms of human achievements, about the possible exploitation of natural energies, etc.), it is not at all this kind of knowledge nor the competence based on it that makes a man educated, i.e. that helps a man to realize his humanity. For this, something else is needed and this something is precisely the real and decisive aspect of human education. The decisive point is that the world as a whole comes into focus. This has been said again and again from time immemorial in the Western tradition: the human mind, like every spiritual being, is by its very nature a receptacle for the whole of reality. But with regard to this totality there is, less than anywhere else, this absolutely exact type of knowledge which is at our disposal for practical purposes. And this limitation in knowledge and control of the world which is *eo ipso* also a limitation of education and educational activity – this limitation we experience in this day and age to an extent that has never happened in bygone times. And it is not uncommon for us to look back enviously to those periods in which the totality of the world and also the totality of wisdom seemed to be within our compass like a brightly-lit room in which a well ordered rich array of treasures is preserved and laid out. Instead, our basic experience of the world as a whole is like that of a man who is down in the depths of the sea in a diving bell and now, as far as the beam of the searchlight reaches and penetrates, more or less clearly discerns and tries to interpret that which stands out against the backdrop of boundless darkness.

I said that we are sometimes tempted to see the distinction between us and the ancients in such a way. But this temptation and this attempt contains, in truth, an illusion, even a twofold illusion. First, our real knowledge of the world is not more incomplete but incomparably richer than that of any earlier generation. The diversity of what we know and of the things of which we have completely exact experience cannot be reduced to a common denominator, and it is precisely these things that prevent us from gaining an overview of the whole. This may seem to us fairly plausible and obvious. But the second point is not at all obvious – the second illusion. The ancients, by which, of course, I don't merely mean people in the past but the great ones, the great witnesses above all of the Western tradition – the ancients completely understood the shell of the world that they knew and which for them was lit up, as an area surrounded by impenetrable darkness and certainly not one on which human knowledge could throw any light, although their successors, classicistic imitators, saw this shell as a brightly-lit room full of treasures. And so the final word of Platonic wisdom is the often misinterpreted saying of Socrates: "I know that I know nothing." This is not meant as an undifferentiated statement of agnosticism. Socrates would not dispute any historian's or physicist's claim to have arrived at completely reliable conclusions; and when he himself is asked: "Do you really know anything, is there something that you know?" he answers very emphatically: "Yes, indeed, I even know a lot!"; but he adds: "Those are mere trifles." And this is exactly the experience of the great teacher of the as yet undivided

149

Christendom, Thomas Aquinas, who has often enough been characterized as a rationalist system-thinker who is never embarrassed for an answer. Thomas knew, also by experience – and he did not withhold it even from the beginners whom he envisaged as the readers of his *Summa* – that the essence, the heart of things remains unknown to us, hidden from us, and that, above all, our knowledge of God achieves its zenith when we become certain that we have no knowledge of God. And so it remains to be said that, doing without comprehensive understanding and any closed philosophical system of the type that filled our grandfathers and fathers with pride – this limitation required of us by experience of reality itself, and this unavoidable helplessness, suddenly places us at the side of the great men of our own tradition. We are completely of one mind with them in the conviction that, in truth, we do not "possess" the totality of the world, that we do not really possess that for which, by our very nature, we are created.

Is education, then, as knowledge about the world as a whole, not an unattainable goal and is, consequently, educational activity a fundamentally impossible task – which, however, must be constantly carried out and provided? It is seen in most average practical everyday affairs: how the individual branches of exact, specialized knowledge are inadequate – no matter how reliable, widespread or even complete they are. We see, for example, how the guidelines for the ethical way of life that we are every day obliged to lead have simply no justification at all if not from an overall view of the world and of human existence. How else could I be able, in all seriousness, to value freedom above my material standard of living? How else could I be alive to and able to deal with

150

the ever present possibility of death? How else could I know what are the decisive human presuppositions for the exercise of political power, the holders of which we are to decide on through our vote? And so on. For all of these decisions repeatedly expected of everyone, a suitability is obviously required which exceeds every specialist and professional competence. It is a suitability which means that the person himself, as person, is right. And part of this is, by definition, that he knows – in whatever way – how things are in the world. And here attention is again focused on the person who teaches – not the teacher of a subject, not the Latin teacher, not the mathematics teacher, not the economics teacher, but simply the "teacher." It is, as one sees, the figure to which this house is committed in a particular way – which, of course, does not mean that the "teacher as such" is not to be found – and must not be found – elsewhere, in the universities, in the secondary schools, the technical schools and, naturally, in human society at large, outside of teaching institutions.

And so it is to this figure – the one who, as such, is the teacher of others – that we look when we ponder the impossibility and, at the same time, the necessity of human education. How does he manage to fulfill the task allotted to him? No one can dispense him from it, just as he has not, to be exact, been given the task by any human authority, for example an education authority. He is familiar with it and entrusted with it by virtue of the nature of things – namely, that he has to do with people who have reason to listen to him. And that is how the inner duty to teach and also the claim (to be taught) comes about. So again: how do we teachers start to do what is our task by the nature of things, namely, to pass on to those learning and listening some idea of total reality and life as a whole when it is, as we must today in all honesty admit, beyond our own grasp? That is, I think, one of the fundamental questions asked of any philosophical theory of teaching as fully human education.

I would like, however, immediately to dispel any fear that might arise that I could be planning now to give an academic lecture on this subject. One must, indeed, give an outline of a philosophical notion of man in order to make clear that the important thing is to keep in its purity an openness regarding the totality, a patient, hoping openness with regard to the undiminished totality of being. This applies not just to the listener and the learner. It is to be achieved ever anew by the teacher – which means doing without the comfortable, rule-of-thumb formulations about the world. As I said, there is no need to expatiate on this.

But I would like to make comments about two things, both of which are equally distinctive characteristics of this house and of our pedagogical institutes as a whole. It is not as if we are talking about something that is always the case and happens, so to speak, of itself. We are dealing with possibilities, with two very special chances, both of which can be implemented – or missed and wasted.

The first chance: keeping total reality present to the human mind – whether as just a presentiment, which, however, demands respect by virtue of its reality – this first chance, which is a distinguishing characteristic of our work in the pedagogical institute, seems to me to consist in the fact that we are dealing with our *mother tongue*, which means that, in our specific task of preparing future teachers for their vocation in our schools, we are required to convert into the physical shape of the German language not only the multilingual corpus of our Western intellectual inheritance but also the findings of modern science which can, in the beginning, only be grasped by the use of an artificially abstract symbolic language. And it is precisely here that we find the very opposite of a limitation or inferiority – by comparison with, for instance, the universities. Here is a chance, which is hardly likely to be found elsewhere, to contribute to the realization of properly human education.

Speaking is always to someone and about something. Therefore language always has two aspects: it is a means of communication and it is access to the world and its reality. Now it seems that we can communicate in every language of which we know the vocabulary and syntax – whether this is our mother tongue or an additional foreign language we have learnt. Nothing seems more obvious to us in this era of international encounter. However, a treacherous illusion can easily come into play here. We have to ask whether access to reality is equally possible in whatever available language we acquire. And the answer has to be: the depth of the world is revealed to us, as a rule, only in our mother tongue – at least that depth of which we have a presentiment of the world as a totality and unity. But that is the same depth in which we experience the really crucial insights into life and in which human education takes place. Hans Freyer once maintained that a person who grows up in the spiritual ambiance of a dialect – in the most intense mother tongue atmosphere – is superior to one who grows up in the thinner air of the written or standard language. The latter person is even damaged, of course not in respect of his ability to communicate in ordinary practical things but in his ability to gain access to reality as such. That is undoubtedly a highly exaggerated formulation, and Freyer probably intended it to be so. But I seriously think that a danger – but also a chance – is being flagged here. The danger, as is obvious, does not lie in the fact that people learn foreign languages but in the reduction of spoken language to what is internationally intelligible and, above all, in the increasing suppression of the spoken mother tongue, with its roots in dialect, in favor of a cheap and shallow paper language. The danger is that all of this could impede or even prevent proper human education. Here we are not dealing with something irrational, I think, but with the very foundations of the *ratio* itself. What is at issue here is not at all the cult of dialect or of national character, nor is it merely a pedantic concern for the purity of language. No, the issue is the spiritual life of man as such – both the highly educated and the less educated. Man's contact with the world as a whole threatens to be impoverished and to shrink if his mother tongue loses its influence. If anyone sees this as playful exaggeration or too unrealistic, or thinks that the danger is not threatening enough, it is possible to point out more drastic things: he may, for example, ponder the almost political question of whether perhaps our continuing insecurity and proneness for arbitrarily and artificially imposed norms is not very closely related to, if not completely identical with, our susceptibility to the purpose thinking of tyrannical powers. Such proneness is certainly intensified by the ousting of the languages we grew up with.

And the chance related to this threat that affects the whole gamut of our life as a community is precisely the distinguishing characteristic of our pedagogical institutes and hardly needs to be mentioned again. It is both chance and task: to keep open the channels of access to the depths of the world through the active cherishing of our mother tongue – in a completely unromantic way, without any provincial narrowness or pedantry, but in collaboration with all men of both the natural and poetic word.

The second chance which must be briefly mentioned here lurks behind the somewhat sinister term relating to the "confessional character" of this institute. Here, too, we are dealing with the very opposite of a limitation to something specialized, to a partial aspect; just the opposite of a limitation of freedom or "intellectual horizon," or whatever. I am almost embarrassed to highlight this to you. Naturally we are dealing with luck and a chance, a prospect of gain – again in the context of achieving really human education, which is in no way able to flourish without exposure to the world as a whole. Of course, this is a chance which can equally be taken up or wasted and ruined. And I do not think it can be taken for granted that this chance will not be wasted. I even ask myself whether as a rule it *is* taken up and used. The aim is none other than to form what we know and what we believe into an image of the world and of existence, richer and with deeper dimensions, but which even so is still, of course, a highly fragmentary image. But this fusion does not come about of itself, not, for instance, because of the mere fact that the researcher and the teacher is also a convinced Christian. The mere juxtaposition of these elements is not sufficient either to achieve the deeper opening up of reality referred to here or even to make it possible. And in the average case something much worse is to be expected than a mere juxtaposition, especially when one takes both knowledge and faith seriously. It is precisely then that conflicts can be expected. We have to be ready for them, face them, come through them, and fight them out. Moreover, it is not at all the case that the conflict always, or even as a rule, arises from science. There is not just a scientific or, rather, non-scientific stubbornness that refuses to acknowledge secret depths; there is also a theological stubbornness, but which we should also call untheological, namely, the stubbornness that refuses to integrate into the interpretation of God's words of revelation what scientific research lays before our eyes with its ever new and sometimes confusing discoveries. This link we are discussing here is not at all easy to achieve, and yet it is the most natural thing in the world. It comes with the thing itself, i.e. with the life of the spirit, the human spirit. It is not for any individual to pass judgment on the person who claims he does not hear any kind of divine word; but one who does hear, and takes what he hears to be the truth, cannot do anything except relate what he has heard in this way to what he has seen himself and to what he knows himself – cannot do anything, i.e. provided he wants to exist from the richness and the unchecked energy of the spiritual life-impulse, and that means *vis-à-vis* simply everything that comes within our range. Thus we are concerned here with something completely different from the political power-plays and aims of those with confessional interests. The Christian who thinks that way destroys his own, in fact, his only chance. Instead, we are concerned with the task that flows directly from the essence of human education! We just need to inquire of any of the great witnesses of Western tradition for confirmation of this – not just Augustine, who says: "No one should claim to be a teacher if he does not speak of God"; and Plato's Socrates, who, when discussing our ultimate knowledge about existence as a whole, gives the word to those who, as he expresses it himself, "are wise in divine things"; this incorruptible man, inspired by *ratio* in his discussions, ultimately gives the word to Diotima, the priestess, and to the sacred tradition of the myths.

And so, if today education of man, although obviously as urgent as ever it was, still seems to be becoming an increasingly impossible task, it is good – and necessary – to consider that it has not only from time immemorial been impossible, only achievable as an approximation and in a spirit of hope, but that it has also always meant an offer of help and that there have always been chances and still are.

And now it only remains to me, looking out over the front rows of the auditorium, to congratulate the students – not only on the truly regal gifts which are the reason for today's celebration, but above all on their decision to put their lives in the service of human education and to become teachers – not of this or of that – but teachers as such. My words of congratulation mean, more precisely, the following: may they, on the one hand, in order not to lose courage, always have living experience of the necessity of what they do; and on the other hand, may they, in order to be preserved from a sterile schoolmasterly arrogance, never forget how impossible and fragmentary a task they are carrying out. Above all, I wish them the most hearty carefreeness in using all their chances to achieve something that is impossible though necessary.

On Plato's Concept of Philosophy

I would make some effort, if dressed in these festive academic robes, to avoid meeting Socrates – the figure through whom Plato most decisively expressed his opinion about the essence of philosophy, not by characterizing it abstractly, not by way of a definition – but more flexibly, in many voices, indeed inexhaustibly, in an ideal figure. In such an encounter with Socrates I would have to be prepared for a conversation like the following: "What a marvelous stroke of fate that I should come across you, most gloriously-clad one! For quite clearly you belong to that extraordinarily fortunate group of persons who have as their most precious possession wisdom, which is what philosophy is in search of – since with such beautiful certainty you call yourself a teacher of philosophy. Please do not begrudge letting me share in this wisdom of yours. For mine, to put it bluntly, is scarcely worth talking about; it is a highly questionable thing; it is like a dream. To be a teacher in this – that seems to me absolutely marvelous; but as for me, I could not do it. And I must simply admit that I have never been anyone's teacher."

With this fictitious Socratic speech we have arrived precisely at our theme. It is, furthermore, not so completely fictitious. I have tried to formulate it in the most authentic words possible. The last sentence used is to be found word for word in Socrates' speech in his defense, which means that it was spoken in all seriousness, in the face of death – by the same man whom the Christian Middle Ages (an almost outrageous parallel!) named alongside Jesus Christ in the same breath: as one of the great teachers who had in common that they left nothing written behind them.

We have arrived at our theme, I said, for it is none other than the object of the philosophical question which occupies us here. – First of all, the statement, "I know that I know nothing" does not arise from some sort of vague "modesty" or a kind of intellectualist coquetry. These often quoted and mostly misinterpreted words of Socrates should also not be understood as a therapeutic trick by the great educator of men which aims at inducing self-criticism in his partner. Nor does the sentence say that no kind of knowledge is possible for man. Socrates would not say to a physicist, to an historian, to any scientific researcher that they cannot arrive at completely reliable conclusions. And when he himself is asked: "Is there something that you know?" he answers emphatically: "Yes, indeed, I even know a lot!"; but he adds: "Those are mere trifles." (And the sciences, perhaps more especially the most exact sciences, would have to accept these words from Socrates-Plato as applying to themselves: their discoveries necessarily lack what is relevant to man's innermost being; they make him learned and perhaps also "competent," but they don't make him wise – something, by the way, to which even the greatest scientists have never laid claim!) The things that are ultimately important, the knowledge of which would make for knowing as such, would make one wise, precisely this, which is ultimately worth knowing, man is not able to know, at least not entirely; precisely this is the experience of Socrates which he never tires of stating. But that is only one side of the coin. The other side of the coin is this: philosophizing for Socrates-Plato means nothing other than – despite all impossibility of possession – continuing in the hunt for that which is worthy of knowing as such, for the wisdom that makes us ultimately wise.

This is the way the words *"philo-sophia"* and *"philo-sophos"* are expressly interpreted: not even Homer and Solon were in possession of this wisdom; it belongs only to God. And so even the wisest of men are, at the most, to be called *philosophoi*, loving searchers after wisdom – after *that* wisdom, of course, of the kind God possesses!

In this mere sketch of a definition of philosophy (here Plato is expressing, on the one hand, something which came down to him from much earlier times (above all, the name of Pythagoras should be mentioned here), and, on the other hand, this same tradition takes from him, Plato, from the new foundation he provides, a fresh, forceful impulse (his great pupil, Aristotle, will, although of a more "critical" and "realistic" cast of mind, take up the thought and expand it further: not only is the wisdom sought after in philosophy the sole property of God, but it is God himself who, in philosophy, is fundamentally what the philosopher is asking about)) – in this still very summary definition we can already see the greatness of philosophy's plan with the same clarity as we can see its questionable nature; we can see the superior freedom and the uselessness; the ambitious aspect and the necessarily inadequate aspect. But above all it can already be seen that, in philosophizing, something happens, which from a "scientific" point of view, is highly "objectionable," even "impossible," something not socially integrated, something which, in a very annoying way, defies organization. And so on. And, as I have said, Socrates would be the first to concede that these worries and concerns are justified. He would both endorse and reinforce them.

This Socratic statement, or rather this Platonic statement – incorporated in the figure of Socrates and his debates – about the nature of philosophy is now to be interpreted a little more exactly, taking account of its elements. In this I will try to retain as closely as possible Plato's concrete way of speaking. In Plato's work there is, as we know, no specialist terminology – and that, too, has something to do with the theme "philosophy," as Plato himself said when looking back on his life: philosophical insight "can in no way be spoken of in the same way as branches of knowledge." But as soon as we say the words *idéa* and *eidos*, which in Plato's Greek are most vivid visual expressions (this, for example, is said: the inner face of things, visible only to the eye of the soul, but still something visible) – if, instead of that, we say "idea" we have already moved from natural language to the artificial: to terminology.

When we proceed to inquire more closely about the elements of Plato's concept of philosophy, the very first answer for us is: the philosopher is concerned with *reality as a whole* and therefore with *wisdom as a whole*. That is the first thing that Socrates speaks of when he undertakes, in the great dialogue about the state, "to define exactly what we really mean by a philosopher": it is always the case that there is, in truth, a strong longing for a grasp of the totality; the really hungry man is not choosy ("perhaps this, but not that"). "So also we will call *him* a philosopher who is eager for the totality of wisdom – not saying 'yes' to this form of it and 'no' to the other." His soul is always alert, ready to go after the whole, the all-inclusive whole, the divine and the human.

These sentences from Plato's *Republic* contain really conclusive information which is much more precise than one may think at first sight. Every branch of knowledge is constituted as this particular one by formulating an "aspect," a clearly defined question which aims expressly and exclusively at this and expressly not at that. No branch of the sciences inquires about the world as a whole. But philosophy is concerned precisely with this – with the totality in all its aspects. No formulated aspect limits the openness of its gaze to this object. The person who philosophizes à la Plato is so much eye and ear that he does not even interrupt this perceiving silence by expressly asking a question. His one worry is that nothing of the totality be left out, overlooked, concealed, kept quiet about, forgotten. This concern is so distinctive, so very much the *differentia specifica*, that one can say that through it the truly serious philosopher can be identified. Accordingly, it would be unphilosophical formally to exclude any achievable information about reality. – But here we must speak more concretely. Anyone who, as a philosopher, inquires about the nature of man would destroy the philosophical character of this inquiry if he were to say, for example: information deriving from medicine, psychology, and genetics are of no interest to me, since I am inquiring about the "metaphysical essence" of man. He would equally cease to philosophize if he were to say: the religious tradition, according to which, because of some primeval event, man is not really what he could and should have been, does not concern me. The philosophical character of the point of departure of the inquiry would also be destroyed if one were to say: my exclusive interest is in what can be known "clearly and distinctly" and can be critically verified; I only want to know what can be conclusively made evident with exact proofs. Such limiting of oneself to specific kinds of knowledge simply contradicts the meaning of philosophical inquiry.

Philosophizing requires a completely unrestricted view which is incompatible with any reservations. Philosophy capitulates at the very moment in which it sees itself as an academic subject or discipline. The philosopher is not characterized by being interested in the discipline "philosophy." He is interested in the totality of the world and the totality of wisdom. This is Plato's concept of philosophy! – What happens in his dialogs? The question is asked in the Symposium: what is love, fundamentally and as such? Then there are answers from the point of view of the doctor, the scientist, the psychologist, the sociologist; but another person speaks, saying: no one can understand Eros who does not consider, in our salvation history, what has taken place between gods and men – and then he relates the myth of man's original guilt and the fall of man and of the inextinguishable longing of man to regain his original whole and healthy state. And finally Socrates conjures up even the priestly figure of Diotima from whom he has derived the knowledge about Eros from the mysteries: "This is what Diotima said, and I have believed it."

It is clear that particularly the relationship between philosophy and theology is at issue. In discussion of Plato's concept of philosophy it is impossible not to touch on this sensitive issue. It is all the more important to formulate the thesis as exactly as possible. I do not maintain that the philosopher is forced, in Plato's view, by virtue of the nature of the philosophical act, to have recourse to a theological interpretation of the world. But the thesis is as follows: the philosophical point of departure, as Plato understands it, not only does not require, but even forbids, the exclusion from the outset of suprarational information about the world as a whole. Such an exclusion is unphilosophical – because the philosopher is, to say it again, *per definitionem* concerned with the totality in all its aspects.

A second element of Plato's concept of philosophy is contained in the following sentence which recurs frequently in the dialogs: the philosopher, as philosopher, is in pursuit of the "idea of being." As I said earlier: this translated expression too easily puts us on the wrong track – the high-sounding, the bloated, the unreal abstraction – whereas Socrates and Plato speak with incomparable concreteness when they try to make clear what is meant by *idéa* and *eidos*. Among his companions in the philosophical conversations there would have been nobody who did not know what the shuttle looks like that the weaver uses to shoot the thread through the warp. "When now" – this is the maieutic question of Socrates – "when now a weaver's shuttle is broken during work and the weaver sets about to cut a new one – where does he look: at the broken piece, or does he not rather look at the image (*eidos*) on which the broken one was modeled?" Of course the answer is: he looks at that image. Here now we want to speak of the "*idea* of the weaver's shuttle." There is nothing to be said against this as long as we don't forget, and cause to be forgotten, that what is meant is not only something absolutely exact and almost visual, but also something that, precisely, is not separated from the sphere of other things that people say and think. What is meant is obviously the model, the design, "the prior image" [das vorgehende Bild. DF] (in the language of German mysticism). Of course, subsequently the realm of the perceptible and of common knowledge is transcended. According to Plato, at the basis of and prior to everything that is there is a pattern, an original form, a design –not only for the weaver's shuttle and other artificially constructed things, no, also for the natural things of our world, even for man himself; there is an original archetype of the good, right, proper human being by which man can and must orientate himself and by reference to which empirical human reality continually has to measure and correct itself – just as the weaver has to follow a design if a usable "proper" shuttle is to be the outcome. Only if we knew this design of man would we completely know what a human being is. Precisely this is what is said of the philosopher: not that he *achieves* such an insight, but that as a philosopher he is inquiring about the archetypes, about the design not of this or of that, not even about the design of human nature, but about the design of reality as a whole, about the ultimate meaning of the very reality of being. – In the words of Plato, philosophizing amounts to being in pursuit of the "idea of being."

Recently, and somewhat unexpectedly, we have been enabled to see the contour of this Platonic view of the world in quite new clarity – through Jean-Paul Sartre's opposition to it – in an unusually radical way, which, by its very radicality, makes for clarity. Sartre's existentialism means, according to his own definition, precisely this: for natural things and, above all, for man, there is no prior basic design; and *because* there is no design, no preceding image of man, there is no sense in speaking of the nature or essence of man. Sartre also says explicitly why this is the case: because there is no God that could have made the design! – Through this contrast, as I have said, the intrinsic meaning of Plato's view of the world can be more profoundly seen. Plato would not have had the idea of creation, the act of creation in the strict sense. But he consistently related the archetypes of things, the "ideas," to the divine sphere. And he said that, apart from the eye and apart from the presence of visible things, a third element was required for us, in fact, to see things, namely, the light of the sun; in exactly the same way a divine light is required for the eye of the soul to become aware of the archetypes. Above all, we need to refer to the statement of the later Plato, that God is the measure of all things. Here, the concept of measure has to be thought of in conjunction with that of the archetype. – Sartre's ingenious denial suddenly reveals for our contemporary thinking the most profound meaning of these thoughts of Plato and allows us to sense a hidden connection which links them with an idea which Plato was not yet able to think. All of a sudden we understand how legitimate Augustine's interpretation is when he sees the teaching of the divine Logos as the quintessence of all archetypes heralded in Plato's theory of ideas.

Naturally, these necessarily simplified comments about the "totality" and about the "idea of being" are not an exhaustive account of Plato's infinitely many-stranded answer to the question about what the philosopher is concerned with. There is a multiplicity of other names he uses to try and express the object of the philosopher's striving for knowledge: it is what is eternally the same and unchangeable; it is the one and not the many; it is that which makes for bliss; it is order; it is the divine.

And yet, after this fragmentary account it is already clear why Socrates insists that the wisdom which is the object of the philosopher's inquiry and quest can in no way become his own property. We can hardly find it difficult to agree to this: the design of the world cannot be known exactly – not the way we can know exactly and definitively at what level of heat a given metal melts. But then there is another difficulty, namely: what sense can there be in chasing after a kind of wisdom that cannot be tracked down; and: is it not meaningless to ask and discuss questions which, it is agreed, cannot be definitively answered? This objection is raised today, particularly in the Anglo-Saxon world, emphatically and with growing influence, by *scientific philosophy*. It affects every kind of philosophizing that appeals to the authority of Plato, which is the same as saying: almost everything that we have meant by philosophy in the West for the last two thousand years. Here there is a highly explosive set of problems which, however, cannot now be discussed any further.

I would only like to attempt to make the Socratic-Platonic view about "not knowing" slightly more comprehensible. This refers to something very well known and which is open to debate on several fronts. The adversary is, above all, the supposed knowledge, that form of not knowing about which the political philosopher Plato warns us when he says: it becomes a source of great crimes as soon as it becomes linked with power. The "not knowing" of the true philosopher has as its presupposition a positive experience in which he has been confronted with the object – of course, as something which is beyond his powers of comprehension. This knowing "not knowing" contains and has the meaning, therefore, of a well-founded statement about the world; namely, that the world is something unfathomable. It is a statement that expresses an experienced finding. Only someone who has had this experience can be a *knowing* non-knower. It is the intensity of this experience which he himself has had – so Socrates says – that explains, so he thinks, why the Delphic god called him, Socrates, the wisest of men. "Make no disturbance, Athenians" – with these words, in the speech in his own defense, he introduces this provocative communication. It is, in fact, disturbing, not only for the Athenians! But when one looks around it becomes clear that this thought structure – knowing "not knowing" as the highest form of knowledge – was never to disappear out of Western tradition. A sentence of Thomas Aquinas reads: "This is the utmost of human knowledge about God: to know that we don't know God." Particularly the German Nicholas of Cusa passionately advocated the Socratic idea. The *docta ignorantia*, he says, is based on a real meeting with the object; only someone who has looked into the sun knows that its light is beyond the seeing power of our eyes.

One could now object that here there is nothing specifically philosophical. The most exact of sciences is continually experiencing its own limits. One could, for example, refer to the letter in which Albert Einstein says, a few weeks before his death: "If there is one thing that I have learned in the ponderings of a long life, it is this: that we are much further removed from a deeper insight into the elementary processes than most of our contemporaries believe."

Against that objection we could answer: the distinction lies in the fact that science ends where it reaches its limit, whereas philosophy begins at this limit. That is, of course, an exaggerated formulation. But one has to see that even the very first philosophical question cannot be adequately answered, and indeed by its very nature. And as for Einstein's statement, we can hardly take it to mean, for example, that all the conclusions reached by modern physics should be doubted – on the other hand, I ask myself whether the missing "deeper insight" that Einstein speaks of does not perhaps refer exactly to that which, in the "elementary processes," is of interest to the philosopher. Because the philosopher is formally concerned with the incomprehensible dimension of the world, a definition of philosophy can never begin with the words: "philosophy is the doctrine of . . ." For the same reason it is impossible to have a closed system of philosophy. Plato would probably be in full agreement with Hegel's criticism of the dialogic, i.e., non-systematic form of his philosophizing (Plato's "philosophical education" – as Hegel says in his *Lectures on the History of Philosophy* – "was not ready" "to produce really scientific works."). But the ironic answer that Socrates, across the thousands of years, would give to the great systematic philosopher could not be formulated worthily – unless by Plato himself. At the zenith of philosophical self-consciousness that precisely in Hegel seems to have reached a kind of absoluteness. In this period of radical decline one had somewhat forgotten that philosophy is more a negative than a positive concept, and that philosophizing, from its very origin, is not so much answering as questioning. For us, in the meantime, not only have the daring answers of the "speculative" systems of philosophy become implausible. We even have difficulty in thinking that philosophical *questioning* is meaningful. But what does the truly philosophical questioning, searching, being in pursuit mean? Plato gives us to understand that it means, above all, as much as acknowledging that there is a dimension of reality that is simply not attainable by our rational efforts. This kind of questioning is not an intellectual game that the sophists are skilled in, but it is the way, and the only possible way, for the knowing mind to keep his unfathomable object in view and to stay near the mystery of the world – on its heels, so to speak. On the other hand, anyone who, in keeping with "scientific philosophy," says: unanswerable questions are meaningless questions – such a person is no longer dealing with the world as a totality. He has already lost sight of it!

Here we have an indication of what sort of demand, in Plato's view, is made of the philosopher and by what the "philosophical man" can be known. It is, above all, the soul's energy to persevere unswervingly in the living spiritual act of inquiring about the world as a whole and in its depths; it is the continually renewed openness to that which causes amazement, which consists in the fact that there is such a thing as existence at all. And all of this is linked with the resolute claim to the highest level of exactitude. Plato says explicitly that it is an exertion like that demanded of a competitor. Furthermore, the oft misinterpreted statement about mathematics as a presupposition for philosophy belongs in this context. It does not mean that the "findings" of the philosopher should (or even could) be achieved and presented *more geometrico*; on the contrary, Socrates expressly calls mathematical education "the prelude to the real song that is to be learnt" – which, of course, means that without the discipline and precision of formally clear thinking the proper result cannot be achieved. It can very well happen that the proper result cannot be achieved *despite* the most precise thinking technique – because the soul lacks the ability to let itself be affected and because, in its questioning, it lacks the simplicity through which alone the object of philosophizing comes into view and remains there.

In Plato's *Republic* there is an astonishing remark

about how this openness can be endangered; Socrates himself says: "Nothing sounds so strange as this" – namely, that precisely what is helpful is a hindrance. It does not particularly surprise us to find that the hindrances to philosophizing are first of all the "so-called good things": beauty, wealth, bodily strength, "connections," and so forth. And, of course, it is also not here that Socrates sees something so very strange. Still, it is somewhat striking with what directness he says of a young companion – who is perhaps even present – that fortunately a rein has been put on him that keeps him with philosophy, namely, his sickliness which, for example, prevents him from going into politics. This is probably not said in all seriousness, but it is also certainly not merely meant as a joke. The most strange thing, however, is now said with unquestionable seriousness: also courage and prudence and other virtues of this kind could be a hindrance to philosophizing, to philosophical contemplation – although they are part and parcel of our proper image of man! What is being said here? That perfection is not identical with self-made ethical perfection. But something is also being said about the innermost nature of the philosophical act.

We have spoken of the soul's energy to persevere unswervingly in the living spiritual act of inquiring (about the foundation of the world, about the totality, about the archetypes, etc.).This formulation is open to misunderstanding. It could be taken to mean, above all, or even exclusively, a strenuous mental activity that the thinker carries out with self-discipline and on his own initiative. But in reality – and this is what Socrates seems to be hinting at with his use of the word "strange" – in truth it is not a question of an activity but of receptivity, letting things happen to the self. What is meant is an extreme, a seismographic ability to hear, as it were, for which is required not so much strenuous effort as silence that fills the innermost self. This silence cannot be achieved through activity – no matter how disciplined – but can be disturbed by it.

The "difficulty" of philosophizing is not one that can be overcome by purely "intellectual work" – which does not mean that the "effort of forming a concept" is super- fluous. In his seventh letter Plato described a kind of test procedure by which a truly philosophical man can be known and one which provides an answer to that diffi- culty. He tried out this test on the ruler Dionysios. "One has to show men what it is to be dealing with the totali- ty, how many difficulties it has to contend with, and what effort it costs. When someone hears that who is a born philosopher, one worthy of the task, a divine man, he will be convinced that a wonderful road has been shown to him; he will be determined to commit all his strength; he will believe that he could not go on living in any other way." The unsuitable ones will either lose heart and give up, or they will think they know enough already.

Again it will perhaps be said that this applies to all research and for all the sciences altogether. Where is any- thing said about what is peculiar to philosophy? Here I would answer: What is at issue here is the "erotic" char- acter of philosophizing; and that is something particular and distinctive. The analogy between the erotic encounter in the narrow sense and philosophizing finds expression in the Plato's "Symposium" and in the "Phaedros" dialog. This discovery seems to be Plato's most personal property. Eros himself, the daemon, is called an "incessant philosophizer"; and in the myth about the soul being feathered, enabling men to raise themselves to the sphere of the gods, lovers and those who philosophize "in simplicity" appear as the only chosen ones out of all other men.

But what is the meaning of this strange mythical manner of speech? The first thing that should be said is that it does not refer to something loosely "poetic." Just as in the erotic upheaval something happens that is not simply in man's control, so also can the philosophical quest for wisdom not be understood as an act that stems completely from man's initiative. In philosophizing it is not that a superior planning reason encounters a world of "possible objects," to which, according to its various aims, it freely turns. Instead, philosophizing springs from a dissatisfaction that we are not master of and which, independently of us, demands to be overcome. When Hans Reichenbach, one of the leading thinkers of scientific philosophy, writes, "The philosopher seems unable to control his drive to know," he is articulating exactly Plato's view. The difference is only that Reichenbach considers this a lethal argument *against* Plato's concept of philosophy. – We see that here, inevitably, far-reaching problems come into play, for example: whether man must not, by virtue of his nature, ask questions which are beyond his understanding; whether, perhaps, as Pascal expressed it, man himself infinitely transcends man.

At this point the proximity of Eros and philosophy to one another can be again newly formulated: in the erotic encounter with sensuous beauty a passion is aroused which cannot be satisfied in the sphere of the senses; a person who has experienced upheaval through Eros will catch a glimpse of a promise, the nature of which is that it cannot be fulfilled in the only way that he thinks is fitting. So, too, in the very first experience of philosophical amazement (what does that mean: something real?) a question is raised which cannot be satisfactorily answered in the finite world, in other words, which cannot be answered "scientifically."

This impossibility of satisfying philosophical Eros – Diotima speaks of "inordinate" *philosophia* – this essential insatiability points beyond the realm of bodily existence. That means that the philosopher, as philosopher, is, both in a tragic and in a comical way, out of proportion to the reality of "this" world. And it is inevitably the case that this disproportion determines the situation of philosophy within human society. A concluding word needs to be said on this point.

We know how much Socrates seemed to derive pleasure from describing – in ever new, often exaggerated terms – how the philosopher does not fit in: he hardly knows where the town hall is; he has no idea about the competition of the power groups for offices of state; he is completely ignorant of things concerning noble and not noble birth: "and along with all of this, he does not even know that he does not know these things" (he is ironically mirroring himself through self-quotation!). The laughter of the Thracian girl who is mocking Thales when, observing the heavens, he falls into a cistern – this laughter is kept ready for those who devote themselves to philosophy. I don't need to repeat what is generally known. By the way, Socrates does not only speak of the philosopher's foolishness. He, too, is able to laugh; when, for example, people "speak in magnificent words," or when praise is given to despots, then it is the philosopher's turn to laugh – even "in earnest"! But enough of this. It is ultimately not very important to know who is more or less justified in laughing about whom.

It seems more important to inquire, after all that has been said up to now, what positive meaning could be attributed to philosophy in the life of human society. "Philosophy" – as we must hastily note in passing – naturally does not mean a particular group of people, not a committee of "professional representatives" whose social function we would be discussing. Socrates said that the race of true philosophers is not at all easy to identify, "not much easier than that of the gods." And we also have to recall his bitter statement: philosophy suffers its worst slander at the hands of those who call themselves philosophers. And so we are inquiring not about the achievement of a particular institution or group, but about the value that philosophizing itself has – wherever it takes place – for human society.

The Platonist Aristotle expresses the self-evaluation of philosophy where he says in his *Metaphysics* that all sciences are more necessary than philosophy, but none has a greater dignity: *necessariores omnes, nulla dignior.* – The "dignity" of philosophy, however, and the position it deserves within society rests on the fact that it alone can generate an indispensable unrest, unrest vis-à-vis the following question: when we have, with an astonishing outlay of intelligence and work, carried out what is necessary – the satisfying of daily needs for living, the provision of food (in every sense), the safeguarding of our survival – what does a life supported like this amount to? What does truly human life consist in?

To ask this worrying question amid all the perfections enjoyed by people accommodating themselves in the world and to keep this question alive using all the means of an incorruptible and exact mental involvement – that is the real achievement of philosophy and its real contribution to the common good, even though, of itself, it is not able to give a complete answer.

The "Equitable" Interpretation

If it is true that Plato is one of the great and venerable witnesses of Western – or even more generally human – traditional wisdom, it is obviously not enough merely to see Plato's *opus* as a document of the Greek language or even as a monument of Greek life after the Peloponnesian war; it is not even enough to read Plato's dialogs as historical witness to the development of philosophical interpretation of the world or as biographical documents of this philosopher's life lived between literature and politics. Although these, too, are possible ways of occupying oneself with Plato's work – all of them meaningful, useful, perhaps even necessary – they are not sufficient as an answer to the question of what Plato really is and what he has to say, *if* it is true – to say it again – that Plato belongs to the great ones, to the "ancients" in a special sense, whose word one can hold on to in the realm of philosophical wisdom as, for example, in the realm of the exact sciences one holds on to the word of the leading researchers with the newest findings! Of course, who says to us that Plato belongs to the great ones, to sit at whose feet it is worthwhile and proper; to whom we turn in an attitude of silent receptivity – in a word, with the attitude of the listener? Why does Plato, along with Socrates and Aristotle and some others, belong there – and why *not* Protagoras and Gorgias and Epicurus and the old Stoics, why not Plotinus? Naturally, I am not able to take up this question here. As we pose this question it is clear that the answer is based on a great multiplicity of presuppositions. But for the moment we are presupposing the answer as something undiscussable, or at least undiscussed.

If, therefore, Plato is a figure of such paradigmatic status, if, accordingly, Plato's *opus* is to be read as a kind of "book of wisdom," why and how is it not "enough" to read it in the way just indicated – as an historical document of the language, history, biography, and even history of philosophy? The answer: because in this way one is not a listener! I don't contest that that way of dealing with Plato is not a serious and meaningful business; I don't contest that in such a way one can pay great attention, and absolutely does pay great attention, to Plato's work; I do contest whether in this way one is "listening" to what Plato says. I can follow a person's utterances with great attention *without* listening to him. One can very easily occupy oneself with Plato in such a way that listening does not come about, and is even hindered. I said already that such a way of dealing with Plato can be entirely valid, fruitful, helpful. What does not come about is that one hears what Plato wanted to be heard. One can quite well try to find out what Plato was thinking – without listening to what he said. – What is this listening, then? Listening is very much an everyday fact – and so is not listening. Everyone who spontaneously speaks to another would like (naturally, in the normal order of things) to be listened to. What does he expect from the other person? He expects that the partner is "interested" in the content of what he says, and that means that he is also interested in something *other* than the speaker – even before the speaker begins to speak. No one who spontaneously speaks will wish that his listener is formally and exclusively aiming at finding out what he, the speaker, thinks and says. That is not "enough" for the spontaneous speaker. He will naturally want the listener to think about what is said, to examine it, to measure it against what he considers is true. A healthy mind even prefers contradiction and objections to the kind of curiosity that is directed at the speaker as such. Moreover, listening is not in every case worthwhile.

However, in the case of Plato, and that is our undiscussed presupposition, it is worthwhile. This does not mean that a Platonic dialog is a canonical text or that there is nothing in Plato that is "only of historical interest." Of course, listening is not achieved by someone who does not have any inner interest in what is being spoken about. Anyone who does not really, with existential seriousness, ask the question to which Plato tries to supply the answer, is not in any proper sense able to listen to the answer. Or anyone who reads Plato formally with a view to being able to say at the end: "this is Plato's opinion about the matter"; or "this is Plato's late style"; or "these are Pythagorean or Orphic inclusions in Plato's thought" – such observations and investigations are, let it be said again, completely meaningful; they are, perhaps, even a presupposition or a help to true listening – but whoever reads Plato with this as his exclusive or primary aim is not thereby listening to him. To put it differently: whoever does not measure Plato's words against what he himself holds to be true or probable; whoever does not look – apart from at Plato – at the objective situation, at the truth, at what he, the reader, thinks is true, is not listening in the way in which Plato himself would expect. To say it differently again: whoever, in reading Plato or any of the other great teachers of wisdom is only out to see what others have thought instead of seeing what the truth of things is, is not really listening to the author, no matter how highly he thinks (or pretends) he esteems him.

To have such a truly listening and thereby philosophizing attitude is the only way of complying with what a figure such as Plato can demand of us by virtue of his status. And it must immediately be added: this way of reading Plato is at the same time the truly formative one; through it alone is a man truly enriched; this is what one must wish above all for young people – precisely because only in it does Plato himself, as a teacher of wisdom, come before us with what is peculiar to him and, so to speak, "come into his own." Of course, another observation cannot be suppressed at this point: the habit of considering the texts from an historical and text-critical perspective has somewhat impeded the spontaneity of that listening approach. I would not go as far as Rudolf Borchardt, who, in his letters to Hugo von Hofmannsthal, speaks – with regard to Pindar – of a certain kind of irreverence as of an "organic error committed even by subtle philological minds": "even the best philologist" believes in other ways of experiencing the divine, "for instance, of shaking the divine by the hand and thanking it for its outstanding achievements." This is quite clearly an exaggeration and is meant as such; the true philologist, as lover of the word, the "*logoi*" and also of the "logos," is much closer to the philosopher than to the historian. But this exaggerated formulation indicates the danger which comes naturally with the attention focused on the *way* the statement is made: the danger, namely, that one thereby forgets to listen to what is said. And yet I think that the whole respectable and admirable endeavor of historical and philological study only comes truly and properly to fruition when it helps us to find a "second innocence" (we don't want to and cannot return to the "first innocence" of medieval and pre-modern interpreters) – a "second innocence," therefore, of belonging even more and better to Plato and "the ancients" as a whole.

Of course, this "second innocence" of spontaneous hearing and reading which is not concerned, in reading Plato, with really finding out what Plato thought but "what the truth of things is" – this approach is not easy for us to achieve and to sustain. And it is not only about us, the listeners and readers, but it is also about what is heard and read, about the work and its author, whose greatness has to be seen and tested in this: that that purely listening attitude with regard to them remains meaningfully possible, *despite* the prior critical analysis of the historians and philologists. Is it still possible to read the "Metaphysics" of Aristotle as a fundamental and elementary textbook of the Western mind, even the fundamental book about being as such, in such a listening way – despite Werner Jaeger's research findings? Is it meaningfully possible, after more than a hundred years of Plato philology, to read the "Phaedo" dialog as a pure listener, i.e. for the sake of a deeper knowledge not of Plato but of the material under discussion: the theory of ideas, *anamnesis*, immortality? If the answer is "yes," the true philosophical greatness of Plato and Aristotle would be seen here in triumphal colors. And this, too, would follow: it is exactly the listening preoccupation with Plato and Aristotle, directed towards reality, towards truth, which makes all preoccupation with historical and philological study at all worthwhile.

But is the presupposition valid? Can, for example, "the immortality argument from memory," on which the whole line of argument in *Phaedo* rests, be seen by today's reader as anything but "purely historical"? Let us quickly recall Plato's thought. If we put it in syllogistic form it looks something like this: learning is fundamentally renewed memory; we remember something that was known and that occurred *earlier*; that which we remember when we are learning and experiencing is *prior* to all experience because the first experience already has the inner form of memory and because what we remember is not to be found in the world of experience; *therefore* the soul already has existence before this bodily existence and is therefore immortal. – And now our skeptical question: how can I, as a modern reader, listen to this argument without at the same time contradicting it and simply turning away from it? How on earth can the real situation become more deeply clear to me through my taking up this thought? In my intention to find out something about the truth of things, how can I read *Phaedo* now that it is completely impossible for every modern person – not just for the Christian, though especially for the Christian – seriously to entertain the idea of the pre-existence of the soul and now that thereby the whole immortality argument collapses along with any justification for speaking of "memory" as the basic form of all learning and of experiencing the world?

Before attempting an answer, I venture to suggest introducing into philosophical interpretation a concept which is commonly used in the sphere of judicial interpretation of legal texts. I am referring to the concept of *epikia*, "equitableness." As we know, it means that a decision is made *contrary to* the letter of the law but in accordance with the mind of the legislator – in a case where a situation arises which the legislator had not envisaged and could not have foreseen. Such an interpretation corresponding to equitableness, is – according to the classical theory of justice – despite its departure from the letter of the law, a higher realization of justice than a literal but non-sensical following of the law. Something analogous could apply, I feel, also to the interpretation of a philosophical text, to its philosophical interpretation. It seems to me possible, on principle, and given certain presuppositions, to do "justice" to Plato in a higher way by *not* keeping to the letter of his text. The historian and the philologist will, I can well understand, cringe at this point. But I have added an important proviso: "given certain presuppositions" such an "impossible" procedure is, however, possible. These presuppositions can be characterized analogously to the presuppositions of the judicial *epikia*: where, in a way which the author could not predict, something which he considered valid is, in fact, not valid! In such a case – this is my suggestion – it has to be possible – even meaningful and perhaps even necessary – to salvage the real meaning of the text by at the same time surrendering the literal meaning. Again: here the most extreme caution and care are required; and, of course, every step in such an interpretation has to be justified "historically" and "philologically." But precisely this distinguishes living tradition from purely historical knowledge: that the exactness of quotation is a secondary value where there is question of the truth at issue becoming more profoundly accessible or not. Augustine sees himself as a loyal interpreter of Plato when he interprets the "ideas" as archetypes of things that dwell in the divine Logos, in the *ars Patris*. One could almost say: as long as an author has a living influence he will be quoted inaccurately because his word is involved in direct participation. Naturally, that is an inordinately exaggerated formulation and is open to misunderstanding. And

183

of course we cannot – as if the hundreds of years of historical criticism had not taken place – return to the not unappealing naivety with which, for example, Albertus Magnus corrected Plato and straightforwardly "complimented" him. What I have in mind here, with regard to Plato and the *Phaedo* dialog, is nothing of this kind. Then what? I have in mind to suggest that we "surrender" the statement about the "pre-existence of the soul," although it is undoubtedly to be found word-for-word in Plato's work. We should ignore it so as to salvage for ourselves the truth of what he really meant. Let us look at this more closely.

Learning should not be learning but remembering. If we attempt to listen to this sentence "unhistorically" free of all the connotations we are familiar with from the history of philosophy we will immediately be surprised about the strangeness of what has been said. Does the sentence have any demonstrable meaning? I learn a foreign language – what do I remember in this? I read, as a non-specialist, a research report about the original inhabitants of Australia or a book about the metabolism of a plant cell – where is memory in that? What could I have already known about it? Is it not simply a thought construct to make such a supposition? But this is not what is meant! Socrates himself cites examples; in the "Menon" dialog, as is known, a young slave is summoned who has had no school education. Socrates teaches him a mathematical theorem without doing anything but ask questions, and the questioned slave gives the correct answer. How does he know the answer? A person opens his eyes, looks at the world, and says: "How beautiful!" How does he know what "beautiful" means? How does a person know what "good" means? He looks and sees that two things are the same – from where does he derive the concept "same"? "Before we began to see, to hear and to use the other senses," we read in *Phaedo*, "we must necessarily have received knowledge of the concept of 'same' from somewhere." Obviously there is, independently of our experience, knowledge about fundamental things, the fundamental structure of reality, the ultimate meaning of the world, the meaning of existence: how does this fundamental knowledge, this beginning, this *principium* on which all learning depends, come about? That is the question which confronts Plato. It is a question to which we do not "in the meantime" have the answer (on the basis, for example, of the fact that we are more than two thousand years "further on"?). The medieval master, Thomas Aquinas, also speaks of a knowledge that comes to us not "from outside," not from the world of objects, and not from experience of this world – from where, then? And even in the "Philosophical Studies" [unpublished in his lifetime. DF] of the logician Ludwig Wittgenstein we read: "If one could imagine this situation: a person remembers something for the first time in his life and says, 'Yes, now I know what remembering is, what remembering is like,' how does he know that this feeling is remembering? . . . Does he know that it is remembering because it has been evoked by something in the past? And how does he know what past means? A person learns the concept of the past by remembering." (If it is by chance that Plato's key concept has been used here as an example of itself, this chance seems to me a very highly meaningful one.) – If, therefore, Plato understands this knowledge of fundamental things that everyone knows about by nature (Caspar Nink's recently published "Ontology," reflecting a Thomist perspective, says that all philosophical interpretation of the world and of being is nothing but a conscious explication of what the person already knew anyway and that, accordingly, philosophy is something quite secondary) – if Plato understands this knowledge of fundamental things as the possession of something forgotten (what is forgotten is still within the reach of the mind; to have forgotten is something more, something more positive, more promising than simply not knowing), and if Plato has used the term "memory" for the regaining (in no way to be thought of as effortless) of this possession which is not simply present to us (in Plato's view, *much* is required for it to be successful: the teacher, for example; a most disciplined review – even reform – of one's inner self, and not at all, as Kant seems to have understood Plato, a rapturous hearing and enjoying of the "inner oracle") – if Plato has called this "memory," his naming of it is ingeniously telling and exact, and just as ingeniously simple. And what is there about it that would only be of "historical" interest? There would not be the slightest cause not to listen any further for the sake of seeking a deeper clarification of things and a clearer grasp of the structure of intellectual life! There is not the slightest reason to look over Plato's shoulder instead of sitting at his feet!

But this is not all that remains despite the surrender of the idea of the soul's pre-existence. Even as an argument for immortality the theory of the memory retains its weight as proof and foundation. Namely, however we conceive of the pre-existence and foreknowledge of fundamental things in the soul, and however one understands the way this "knowledge of genuine reality" comes about – in any case what is said is that the soul, prior to all experience in this life, is privy to the realm of truth in a very special way. Plato speaks of the "ideas"; that the "ideas" are pre-knowledge, the things we have normally forgotten, but also what can be remembered, what can be recovered by way of memory. But the "ideas" – however we want to define more accurately this concept of Plato's – are for Plato doubtless something that belongs to the sphere of the divine. Sharing in these ideas therefore means sharing in an intensity of being that transcends the limitations of the finite – just as it is true of memory that in this act the soul makes contact with its own unfathomable foundation (something that the Platonist Augustine never tires of contemplating anew: "Great, oh God, is the strength of my memory, enormously great, a silent sanctuary, wide and limitless," as he says in Book X of the *Confessions*; and it is the strength of human memory to which the famous sentences of the same chapter refer: "Men go and look with astonishment at the peaks of the mountains, the unlimited waves of the sea, the broad flow of mighty rivers, the endless expanse of the ocean, and the course of the stars – yet they don't see themselves or they see themselves without being astonished.") But if, as Plato was seemingly the first to say, the human soul is of such a kind that the beginning of knowledge comes about in contact with an indestructible, suprahuman light (a beginning with which we find ourselves in communication through the power of memory) – if the soul is of such a kind, then it is likewise indestructible. This means: the thesis about the memory character of our knowledge can also then be considered an argument for immortality when what is said word-for-word in *Phaedo* ("thus we must have received this knowledge *before we were born*") is given up.

Whatever else constitutes the foundation of the greatness of historical figures: we will only count a *teacher of wisdom* as one of the great if his teaching, transcending all historical conditions, has the power – also for modern readers – to open up the world and to throw light on reality. But this strength, this real gift and "message," will only be glimpsed and possessed by one who, in dealing with texts and documents, is primarily concerned with "finding out the truth about things as they are."

Platonic Figures (I)
Callicles: The Man with No Rapport with Truth

It is astonishing that Plato, this ancestor of all Western philosophy, seems to have written only dialogs in the course of his eighty years – no text books and treatises like the ones we are used to today, but conversations in which he brings together human figures which are vividly and concretely drawn. If this is not a purely external coincidence, then it surely means that Plato expressed what he had to say through figures and not through theses, propositions, and argumentations. It means that, for example, it is not possible to formulate Plato's theory of Eros in abstract propositions which would allow the logical conclusion that here is – without the omission of anything essential – what Plato has said in the *Symposium*. Whoever wants to hear what Plato intended to say in his work must not only pay attention to the factual arguments of the dialogs but also to the behavior, to the attitude, to this extremely differentiated structuring of the gestures of the partners in discussion – otherwise he simply does not come to see anything of Plato's statement.

In his figures, Plato did not merely present the bearer of certain opinions, but in them he presented, I believe, the embodiments of living, real attitudes that people had with regard to truth. A man relates to truth not only the way the knower relates to his object. The true is not only true, but it is also good. Truth is something worth striving for; it concerns not only the intellect, but also the will, not only the head, but also the heart. That means that man relates to truth as a living, *active* being – and therefore with all the possibilities not just of error, but also of doing wrong, of confusion, of degeneration, of perversion! For example, it is possible for someone to say: truth is irrelevant for the man who has to act and be practical. The man of action is not "interested . . . in the truth of things." What interests him is power, wealth, honor, pleasure. To assert himself, "to stay alive," to achieve his aims – *that* is what interests the practical man, but not truth. This is an example of what can be said and would be one possible attitude towards truth – a negative possibility: that of the untheoretical person who has no rapport with truth! And perhaps it is useful to begin with such a negative figure which embodies the perversion of man's relation to truth – for example, Callicles in Plato's "Gorgias" dialog.

Callicles is a somewhat puzzling figure; we don't know of any historical Callicles. On the other hand, it is not exactly likely that a figure of such weight and so clearly and vividly sketched would be a complete invention. It has been thought, with good reason, that Plato has here portrayed Alcibiades – under a pseudonym, so to speak. But this question is not so important for us. The outline of the Callicles figure is clear enough in any case.

The "Gorgias" dialog has three parts. Callicles speaks only in the third part, in the "last act," as it were, after he has listened to the conversations of Socrates with Gorgias, the sophist, and Polos, the pupil of the sophist. The theme of these conversations is: power/powerlessness, right/wrong; one can also say: the power of wrong, the powerlessness of right. Gorgias and Polos are teachers of rhetoric, i.e. they are "intellectuals"; Callicles, on the other hand is a speaker [Rhetor. DF], i.e. politician, a man with power, a pragmatist. Without saying a word, he lets the conversation of the intellectuals pass until Socrates' radical, absolutely fearless insistence on the truth – which makes the sophists wilt – and his own (i.e. Callicles') absolutely fearless and radical stance of the ruthless power pragmatist provoke him to debate. In the end – in the conversation between Socrates and Polos – there was talk of the powerful; Polos speaks of them with admiration. Socrates says that, for his part, he considers them worthless: they do what they think is good, but they don't do what they "really" want; and therefore, to be exact, they are not powerful: "In a state, a man can do what he thinks is good and still not possess great power." Polos is confused by this statement. He suspects that behind it there is more than purely dialectical skill, namely, an invincible, existential radicalism. This is where Callicles intervenes. He turns first to Socrates' companion: "Tell me, is Socrates being serious, or is he joking?" The last thing Socrates had said was: to *suffer* injustice is not so bad as to *do* injustice. Callicles seems to be very interested in this distinction "seriousness/joke." For him, seriousness seems to amount to "theoretical dialectic of the sophists," abstract utterance, "philoso-phy"; whereas "seriousness" seems to be what works in practice. And that is what is both unbelievable and at the same time something that has become worthy of belief through Socrates' attitude: that such an opinion – to com-mit injustice is worse than to suffer it – can "seriously" be entertained, not just in books and as accepted theory; an opinion which – as Callicles himself formulated it – "would turn real life and its daily practice, our entire daily life, upside down." – Socrates takes up the chal-lenge: the decisive factor that distinguishes him from Callicles is, in fact, not merely an opinion; the decisive factor is to be found in Eros, in the orientation, from the centre of our existence, to reality as a whole: I am one who loves philosophy, but you are one who loves the people of Athens: "When you are speaking in an assembly of the people and the people express a different opinion, you change, and now you say what they want." "But philosophy says always the same thing" – philosophy stands for truth insofar as we can grasp it – "and if you do not agree with philosophy, with truth" (this is how Socrates concludes the first speech with which he attacks the heart of his adversary), "then, dear Callicles, Callicles is not in agreement with you." That has to mean: whether you know it and like it or not, truth is related to man's very being, and when you are opposed to truth you are opposed to yourself!

Callicles answers by trying – speaking more in a monolog than giving a real reply – to formulate his own opinion, similarly from within himself: what matters is to be strong – *that* is the only adequate answer to the true reality of life. I don't take talk about law and justice seriously. Looking at it without illusion: it is the attempt of the weaker person to find some advantage for himself. But philosophy, the striving after truth and wisdom, *theoria* (defined as follows: focused on truth and *nothing else*) – "philosophy, dear Socrates, is indeed very nice and has a certain attraction when one is engaged in it in one's early years"; however, if one engages with it more deeply it becomes harmful, because it hinders one from learning what is needed in the world for asserting oneself. "When I see a man who has reached mature years and is still philosophizing – such a man, dear Socrates, deserves a beating: that is my opinion." "For example, is it wise, my dear Socrates, not to be able to help oneself? One could, if it does not sound too rough, slap such a man's face with impunity."

Here we see the real contrast brutally expressed: on one side Socrates, the man who incessantly searches after truth, who knows and states that man is nourished by truth – not just as one who knows, but as one who desires to *live* as a human being; on the other side, there is Callicles, who says: whatever about the essence of things: that is something that gives nothing to and takes nothing from the man of action; one can even say: one *may not* worry about truth if one has goals to reach. A principle is involved here: not merely that, in practical life, one sometimes has to allow five to be an even number; that in the fights of the working day we need to be less concerned with commitment to objective truth; but: that theoretical truth has, on principle, nothing to do with the achieving of our aims. Yet Plato, on the other hand, seems to have been the first to express the wise insight of Western – or, rather, simply human – thinking: that all human praxis is measured, judged and legitimized by confrontation with reality.

Callicles' position, as it is easy to see, is the continuing possibility of human degeneration, a position of validity (or invalidity) that transcends time. In his novel *Brideshead Revisited* Evelyn Waugh portrayed a modern Callicles, a successful, intelligent, ambitious businessman in middle-class England between the two wars. This Mr. Mottram aims to marry a rich and beautiful girl from the Catholic aristocracy and he decides, for different social and business reasons, also to become a Catholic. Since no one has influenced him in this, everyone assumes that there will be no problems with his "conversion." He is recommended to a Jesuit who is experienced in these things and who undertakes to instruct him. And after some time this priest declares, to everyone's surprise and embarrassment, that Mr. Mottram is the most difficult case he has ever had to handle. – Yes, but is he not determined to be received into the Church? – Precisely this is where the problem lies; what is peculiar to this vigorous desire is the very source of the impediment. Mr. Mottram, in the experienced priest's formulation, cannot be aligned with "any kind of heathen known to missionaries." "On the first day I wanted to find out what sort of religious life he had lived up to the present, so I asked him about his idea of prayer. He replied: I have no idea at all. *You* tell me. I attempted it in a few words, and he said: right, so much for prayer. What is next? – I gave him a catechism. Yesterday I asked him whether there is more than one nature in Our Lord. He said: exactly as many as you say there are, Father." Mr. Mottram himself is completely surprised that anyone could find an impediment in his attitude. ("One would have thought you would be happy to have a man like me – instead of which you are acting like people who give out cards for an exclusive casino.") With regard to the explanation of the *truths* of faith, he said: "Instruction is lost on me. Simply give me a form and I will sign on the dotted line!"

This Mr. Mottram is, without doubt, not simply stupid; he is also not without sincerity. He is not deceiving himself or anyone else with regard to the real motives for his "conversion." Something very fundamental is incurably wrong – but *what* is it? The Jesuit sums up his argument like this: "This man seems to have no sense of reality." Having no sense of reality does not mean here that he is incapable of understanding a situation, sensing where the opposition lies, where the problems are, what opportunities are available and weighing them up in relation to one another. It means that he does not see or deny that it belongs to the nature of human activity to come at it from the *ipsa res*; that it is part of the nature of decision to be the *translatio*, the translation of what we perceive to be real, of *theoria*. On the other hand, to see this means: as a man of action to have a sense of reality.

It is, moreover, easy to see that here we are not simply dealing with an "interesting figure in a novel." Such a perverse relationship to truth largely defines the political reality of our age. All the totalitarian regimes of the present have in common that the world views and "teachings" proclaimed in their programs cease to have any binding force as soon as they threaten the wielding of power. Memoirs about the internal affairs of regimes that are now crumbling are full of evidence of this. Ignazio Silone reports that at an international conference of functionaries the suggestion was made formally to accept and publish a particular resolution but then, in practice, to *do* exactly the opposite. *One* voice was raised against this, a truly Socratic voice, a voice for truth – a voice which, as Silone reports, provoked "a storm of hilarity"; and Silone adds: "This general laughter showed the full significance of the timid objection." What is happening here is not just lying. What is happening is a statement that there is no distinction at all between truth and falsehood.

But we are speaking here of Plato's figure; we are speaking of Callicles. Although at first sight the modern figure in the novel is different from the powerful politician of the ancient city state, although in the concrete there seems a difference: fundamentally we are dealing with figures of the same type of degenerate attitude towards truth! A philosophical conversation with Mr. Mottram is no more imaginable (for instance, a conversation about the fundamental nature of piety – a very Platonic theme) than a philosophical conversation with Callicles would be possible. And if, in the extremely lengthy dialog between Callicles and Socrates, one does not see this impossibility; if one does not become aware of the despair which characterizes the depressing atmosphere of the conversation; if, like all the commentators, one only looks at the factual content without seeing that this only *appears* to be a conversation – which in reality is a monolog spoken to deaf ears, ironically confident in its persistent defiance of all hope –; if one does not look at the *figures*, one misses an essential element of what Plato is saying; it is as if one were to read the libretto without ever hearing the music. Callicles is forced by the situation, or rather by the helpful unyielding attitude of Socrates, not to give up the pretence that a real conversation is taking place. But he is not affected by Socrates' arguments. It belongs to the nature of his position that it cannot be shaken by arguments, by *theoretical* arguments – i.e., those that deal with truth. His position is not based on argument but on a completely *untheoretical* self-assertion which is, on principle, not concerned about truth. Socrates asks: "Do you accept this opinion? Or do you have an objection to it?" Callicles: "No, I accept it so that there will be an end to your proof." Or, a few pages further on: "I don't understand you at all, Socrates. Ask someone else! What you are saying is irrelevant to me." To this Socrates replies: "Fine, what should we do now? Should we break off the inquiry in midstream?" "Do what you like." "But they say you should not break off even fairytales in the middle. On the contrary one should persevere with them . . . ." "Oh, as far as I am concerned drop the inquiry!"

Plato pushes this conflict so far that it finally becomes clear: here we are not only dealing with two extremely different contrary figures; it is not merely about the portrayal of two natures that represent the opposite ends of a series of possible attitudes to truth – at one end of the series the man of *theoria* concerned with truth and "nothing else," and at the other end a man of praxis, concerned with anything but truth. But it is clear that the *existence* of both of these figures, the witness to truth and the man who has no rapport with truth, is intrinsically linked, almost like the hangman and his victim. It is the detached pragmatist, the man of power who is, on principle, not concerned with truth, to whom the witness to truth falls victim. "What are you encouraging me to do," Socrates asks Callicles – "should I be to the Athenians like a doctor who insists that they should be as good as possible, or should I be like a slave who is only concerned with currying favor?" We must hear the threat contained in Callicles' answer: "How secure you seem to feel, dear Socrates . . ., as if you lived apart and as if nothing could happen to you." Socrates answers: "I would really need to be a fool not to know that in our city all kinds of things can happen to a person . . . Also I would not be surprised if, in such a case, death would befall me. Should I tell you why I expect that? As a doctor would be condemned by children if a maker of sweets brought an accusation against him, so will I be condemned . . . *That* is the reason why, whatever it is to be, I will have to let it happen."

The fact that here, in this prelude full of reference, the trial and fateful death of Socrates are explicitly prefigured – precisely this shows us the profound significance of these figures and what they say.

Platonic Figures (II)
The Learners

Who were the real participants in Plato's *Symposium*? The mere enumeration of them caused excitement for the contemporary reader, for whom every single name conjured up an exactly definable human figure. That Socrates is such a figure, and what he meant, is something we are aware of today. But who was Agathon? Agathon is the host of the circle he has invited to his house to celebrate a victory – the victory of the poet Agathon, whose tragedy won the laurel wreath in a competition. He is a pupil of the sophists; a rich, handsome, clever man of the world, somewhat smug, sensitive to the slightest fluctuations in public esteem, very susceptible to applause and its various levels; besides, a very "modern" man: he is the first to have *invented* the material for his writings. Moreover, in his *Divine Comedy* Dante praised Agathon alongside Euripides – in hell, of course.

Then there is Aristophanes, of whom every Greek reader of Plato knew that in his comedies he put both Agathon and, above all, Socrates, on the stage as laughable figures. And now this man sits with his victims at the same table. In the case of Socrates we can speak very precisely of a "victim". When Socrates stands before the court he has not only the accusation relating to his trial to deal with but also – as he says himself – a much more dangerous accusation which has been brought against him in Athens for years: "You have seen it yourselves in Aristophanes' comedy how a completely ridiculous Socrates turns a bad situation into a good one, etc." Here in the *Symposium*, Alcibiades nonchalantly quotes a comical reference from this same comedy of Aristophanes, which has, in all seriousness, shared the guilt for his death: " . . . striding in, proud as a peacock and rolling his eyes – to use your well-known words, Aristophanes." This is the way Socrates, as a soldier, is supposed to have been seen on the battlefield of Delion.

Alcibiades likewise appears in extremely sharp contours in this circle: a disastrous figure in the eyes of every patriot, a cynical ruler without ethical restraint, totally dependent on the applause of the masses, whom he, the demagogue, is skilled in rousing. So Alcibiades, he too, speaks in his own way – the way of a drunkard – about Eros. After all the others, after Phaedros, Pausanias, Eryximachos, Aristophanes, Agathon, Socrates – each one of whom, through the quite distinctive sound of his voice, lends to what is said the unmistakable, special music of a real *vox humana*.

But I did not really want to speak now of those who, in speeches, participated in the symposium with their own particular contribution. There are also silent but nonetheless alert and important participants, above all, a still quite young one named Aristodemus. Of course, with regard to being alert, this is not exactly his strength; it is, ultimately, a non-conversation, and there is a lot of drinking; and so the young man can't help falling asleep, and for hours he is not part of the circle, even as a listener. Yet this Aristodemus figure seems to me a figure of special importance to Plato – and if for Plato, then also for us. Aristodemus is one of the youths in Socrates' company, one of the most enthusiastically devoted to the master at the time, as is said. This wild enthusiasm, this uncritical veneration is depicted by Plato in a way which can be described as ruthless: how this barefooted follower – barefooted because Socrates did not wear sandals! –, how this devoted little dog is picked up by his master on the way and brought to the symposium. But Socrates is then suddenly overcome by a thought and, as it were, rooted to the spot, so that Aristodemus comes to Agathon's house without his master, where he is by mistake brought into the celebrating party, stammers out the most helpless explanations and excuses, in extreme embarrassment looks around towards the door, through which, however, Socrates will still not make his entrance; while Agathon, with a laugh, asks where the master is, and with captivating friendliness and an air of complete superiority which now really offends the awkward Aristodemus, invites his chance guest in and forces him to sit down.

All of this is ruthlessly portrayed; however, there is also a positive point which, of course, is not particularly evident. I am referring to the fact that it is Aristodemus to whom we, the readers of the *Symposium*, owe the knowledge of those speeches about Eros and therefore of the deepest thoughts Plato entertained in his mature years: he, Aristodemus, listened and recorded what he heard in a report which he handed on. This, at least, is how it is seen if one looks closely at the structure of the *Symposium* which Plato shaped with unusual care. Aristodemus is a direct reporter. And yet he does not feature directly, not even as a reporter. And we are only told about him by a second reporter. The *Symposium* is the beginning of a series of dialogs in Plato's work which are encoded in this highly complicated, even annoying way: one person reports what another person has told him; and only then, in this high level of mirroring, does the real dialog – what is really meant – come into view.

The second reporter, Apollodorus, is a person similar in kind to Aristodemus; Apollodorus, too, is "crazy," as the Athenians say of him. He is referred to as *manikós* or cracked [*übergeschnappt* in German. DF]. Plato has him describe himself at the beginning of his report: how overjoyed he is to be allowed to speak about philosophy; early he strolled through life like everyone else, thinking he was working wonders, whereas he was in reality simply pitiable – he knows that now for the three years since he met Socrates. With completely wild enthusiasm he has become Socrates' devotee. Every day, as Apollodorus himself says, he is eager to know not just what Socrates is saying but also what he is doing. No one is of any importance in his eyes except Socrates; he rails against everyone, including himself. "Perhaps you think," he lets his friends know when they tell him he is crazy, "perhaps you think I am unhappy; and you are right" (I am not "like Socrates"); "but, with regard to you, I don't just *think* you are wretched and pitiable; I know it with complete certainty."

And such an uncritical, overenthusiastic little student is the one chosen by Plato to report on the speeches about Eros in which he has expressed the essence of his thoughts about the nature of love and the nature of philosophizing. How strange! Does this mean that Plato is here making a statement about the perpetual state of philosophizing in the world? For this, too, is part of the picture: that it is an audience of successful and moneyed people to whom Apollodorus presents those thoughts! Was it perhaps Plato's design to make clear that it belongs to the essence of philosophizing that it take place in the middle of a world which in no way nourishes the search for truth; in the middle of a world, which, on the contrary, has to be surpassed and overcome ever anew in the philosophical act? Does he mean to say, perhaps, that the true philosophizer finds himself in what always seems to be a hopeless situation in which only the persistently youthful search for wisdom, the genuine *philosophia*, can stand firm? – I do believe that Plato, in a distinctive Platonic way – through his figures – wanted to say something of this kind.

But something else as well must be meant by a figure like Apollodorus. Scholarly interpretations seem to overlook it entirely. Apollodorus is hardly mentioned. He is thought to be only a kind of Wagner [assistant of Goethe's Faust. DF] figure, an extra, who is of no importance in himself. But this does not fit together with the fact that Apollodorus is named in a very remarkable way in another dialog of Plato's mature years, the *Phaedo* – though likewise only in a few sentences. They are all, as Phaedo says of Socrates' last day, shattered by the conflicting feelings of sadness, joyful admiration, of parting; and all of them could not hold back their tears: "above all, one of our number: Apollodorus. You know the man and the kind he is." And when Socrates raises the cup of poison to his lips: "My tears flowed," said Phaedo, "in such floods that I had to hide my face and cry, not for his sake, but for my own sake: what a friend was being taken from me! . . . Apollodorus had already earlier not stopped crying, and now he broke out uncontrollably in loud lamentations – and there was not one of us unshaken by him except Socrates himself, who said: 'What are you doing, strange people!'"

The irony with which Plato undoubtedly portrayed Apollodorus elsewhere is not crushing; there is always a sense of hope; there is the kind of understanding one usually has for one's own past: a good-natured ironical understanding, an almost paternal understanding. Sometimes I actually think that Plato might have portrayed himself in these youths in Socrates' company, where he is otherwise persistently silent about himself – with the exception of one occasion! It almost takes my breath away every time, when Phaedo, asked who was present in the cell on Socrates' last day, names them all and then adds at the end: "I believe Plato was sick." I sometimes ask myself whether Plato portrayed himself in these pupils – all of them. Like Apollodorus, he, too, underwent a sudden "conversion"; after his meeting with Socrates which even in his old age he described as providential and the greatest happiness of his life, he threw all of his tragedies into the fire. He was, moreover, approximately the same age as Apollodorus; that, too, would fit. But, be that as it may! Whether in the features of the pupils we are justified in seeing the youthful Plato or not – Plato seems implicitly to have incorporated a very definite meaning in these figures: namely, the way in which, ideally, learning takes place – given the supposition that there is a real teacher, an existential teacher. These figures seem to be saying: learning does not happen by a neutral and critical mind examining and testing what the teacher presents and then accepting or rejecting it. But as Plato's pupil, Aristotle, formulated it: whoever wants to learn must believe; whoever wants to find out the truth about the ultimate, the real, God and the world must turn trustingly to a person – the teacher. That means in a certain sense uncritically, in a silent willingness to listen. Descartes' principle, which refers the individual to his own isolated subjectivity, has blocked our access to Plato's wise view, which the Far East never lost:

namely, that wisdom cannot be had without a personal teacher.

But it is not merely trust that links the youths around Socrates with their teacher: it is love. "One only ever learns from the person one loves" – a saying of Goethe's. I know that it is natural here to think of the forms of Eros which characterized and were peculiar to the Athens of the classical period. But one would misunderstand Plato and Socrates if one were to interpret the teacher-pupil relationship as an erotic love of boys – although the youths philosophizing with Socrates understood him or, rather, *mis*understood him in this way. One of them, the drunken Alcibiades – this same Alcibiades of whom Socrates called himself the lover – said: "Be clear about this: none of you really knows this man! You see, for example, how much Socrates is in love with beautiful boys. Is he not quite like Silenus in this? But it is only the outward shell, precisely like the carved figures of Silenus hide a divine image within. In fact, he is not in the least concerned if they are beautiful or rich. On the contrary, he considers all these things and us, too, to be worthless. What people see of him is pretence, and he has been playing this game with them all his life. Whether anyone else has seen the divine images in him I don't know. But I have seen them." And then Alcibiades relates what only a drunken man could relate: how, in an unforgettable night that he spent with Socrates, he was liberated from and cured of his illusion that Socrates was concerned with eroticism in the narrow sense – a cure which still burned and stung him like the bite of a viper.

Therefore, we cannot take *that* to be their meaning when Socrates and Plato seem to say that the presupposition for learning is found in some sense in love, in loving identification with the teacher. What is meant, on the contrary, is that, through such an identification, such a trick (Nietzsche), the pupil is put in a position where he can see the object as if with the eyes of the teacher; where he makes contact with spiritual realities which, from a purely intellectual point of view, he is not at all able to grasp but which he becomes aware of, however, through that uncritical affirmation of the teacher, through identification with him; not, therefore, on the basis of interest in the subject, but on the basis of his bond with the teacher: *this* is how learning takes place in its most intense form.

What distinguishes the pupil figures is, furthermore, a strange ambiguity, an awkwardness, insecurity, sensitiveness and an astounding unrelatedness to their own goals. They are eager, in an enthusiastic, vehement, and tempestuous way – to learn *what*? They themselves are unable to explain it. There is this young Hippocrates, for example, about whom Socrates relates in the *Protagoras* dialog: on one occasion, at night, "when day was scarcely breaking," Socrates was awakened by this youth knocking on his door with a stick and asking the enormously intelligent question, "Socrates, are you awake, or are you asleep?" "I knew him by his voice and answered: That is Hippocrates! You are not bringing me bad news? – Not in the least, he answered, but good news! – I hope you are right! What is it then, and why have you come so early? – Protagoras has arrived, he replied, as he came in." That is the whole explanation for the breathlessness of this visit during sleeping hours: that the famous orator and wandering teacher, the sophist Protagoras had come to Athens. Socrates pretends not to understand and provokes the impatiently

enthusiastic Hippocrates to give a fully clear explanation of himself. But that is nothing new, says Socrates.
Protagoras arrived the day before yesterday. Yes, that's
right, but he, Hippocrates, only heard about it last
evening! Everything is told in all its important detail:
pursuit of a runaway slave, return "very late in the
evening"; "and now as we had also had our evening
meal and were about to retire to bed, only then does my
brother say to me that Protagoras has come. I was quite
inclined still to go to you, but then I thought it was too
late in the night." Socrates, determined not to understand, still mystified by this excitement ("I knew his
vehement and tempestuous nature . . ."), replied: "But
how does that affect *you*? Has Protagoras done anything
to you?" "By the gods, he has: that he alone is wise and
does not make me wise!" "Oh, he will make you wise, all
right – if you give him money . . ." Hippocrates does not
grasp the lethal irony in this comment. He does not want
to hear it: "If it were only to depend on that, oh Zeus and
ye gods, I would not stint with my own money and with
that of my friends!" And so Socrates is to arrange an
introduction to Protagoras – and immediately. "But it is
not even daytime yet. Until then let us wait and chat."
Socrates now tries to find out what is the point of this
vehement desire for the truth: "We will now both go to
Protagoras and we are prepared to sacrifice our own
money and, if need be, also that of our friends. . . . But
do you know what you are about to do? Or don't you
know?" And it becomes clear that Hippocrates doesn't
know for what he wants to make these sacrifices; he
doesn't know what he really wants! He says he has in
mind to become "a wise man" – and he is immediately
embarrassed and blushes ("There was already a little

daylight, says Socrates, so that I could see it clearly"). Hippocrates then says he wants to have knowledge. But when Socrates asks him what kind of knowledge, he doesn't know what to say. "What is the subject in which the sophist himself is knowledgeable and in which he makes his pupil knowledgeable? – By Zeus, he replied, I couldn't say!"

And this is exactly what Socrates enjoys so much; precisely here is the basis of hope, the chance for this youth Hippocrates – and for all the others as well! At least, that is Plato's view. One only has to glance at the pupils of the sophist, the way they can say exactly what kind of knowledge they wish to acquire; what they intend to "do" with this knowledge; one only needs to look at the contrasting figures of the pupils around Socrates to become immediately aware of the positive, pleasant, profoundly appropriate nature of their disponibility.

Hippocrates, Apollodorus, and Aristodemus are to the sophist's pupils exactly as Socrates is to the sophists. The sophist is not at all embarrassed when asked to define the wisdom he can teach: "Young man – as Hippocrates will hear from Protagoras – on the first day after you have been with me you will return home as a competent man." Socrates, on the other hand, says: "I have never been anyone's teacher"; "my wisdom is like a shadow, even like a dream!" Why this self-deprecation? It has nothing to do with any vague kind of modesty. Socrates, and also the youths around him, these genuine learners, have in mind a wisdom capable of casting light on the secret of the world, knowledge, therefore, with which all true philosophy is concerned. And it is peculiar to this goal that it cannot be described with the definiteness that applies to any practical concrete goal.

And therefore anyone who truly seeks for what is genuine, for the key to the world, to the world that is never completely decipherable, fathomable for the finite mind – every genuine philosopher is a learner of the same kind as Hippocrates, Aristodemus, and Apollodorus!

Conversation as the Place of Truth

Truth, as human reality, comes about only in conversation. Plato says this in his famous Seventh Letter, in which he looks back on a long life of teaching and writing. I shall attempt to say in a few words what, as far as I understand it, he means by this statement.

It refers first of all to the truth which is the object of philosophizing, to the truth, therefore, about the whole of reality and about the meaning of human existence as a whole. What is meant is the truth that makes one wise. None of the individual sciences can lay claim to creating wisdom and "knowledge" as such. Eruditeness and competence are something different from wisdom. Philosophy also does not create wisdom; but "wisdom" is what philosophizing aims at insofar as it is a "loving search." And the insight in which we are confronted with this wisdom – although from a long way off and as something we cannot possess once and for all – this insight, in Plato's view, happens and is realized only in conversation. As if by a flying spark, a light is unexpectedly lit in the soul: *if* people again and again come together and speak with one another "for the sake of truth."

This statement is meant in such a way that it excludes two things. It is directed against the opinion that this kind of truth can be really at home in the written word. Writing and reading are, in Plato's view, not the forms in which truth as human reality is primarily realized. That is a somewhat strange statement in the mouth of a man who operated certainly for more than fifty years through the written word! The most surprising thing is that this same man insists that he has written nothing about the things which are of importance to him. And the man who tries to express in writing his most serious thoughts, that man's heart must have been destroyed, not by the gods, of course, but by men.

Plato's estimation of conversation is opposed, furthermore, to monolog – something, therefore, to which we have become accustomed in teaching. Again and again Socrates implores his sophistic conversation partners: don't make a speech but agree to converse with us! – It can, of course, be shown that Plato and Socrates are not really referring to the merely external fact of "speaking alone" but to the inward "partnerless" speaking, in which the speaker alone is "on stage," while the listener is not acknowledged as a partner of equal standing but is either simply ignored or is reduced to being the mere object to be affected.

I don't believe that we should simply accept as "true" these deliberately exaggerated formulations of Plato; but it is worth thinking seriously about them – as a contribution to the theme "conversation."

On Plainness of Language in Philosophy
Notes on C.S. Lewis

Not everyone would, I think, see C.S. Lewis's book *The Problem of Pain* as light reading. But no one can dispute that its author's style of writing is a model of clarity and plainness. This humorous, handy kind of expression is found often enough in the English-speaking world. In guest lectures in the U.S.A. I often experienced the beneficial difficulty that this language resists everything that is vaguely abstract. "Many will say: if things cannot be more clearly expressed than they are by Heidegger and Jaspers one would do better not to try and say them at all" – this bold sentence, which appeared recently in *The Times*, can be deemed typically Anglo-Saxon. Of course, it does point a little to the boundary set by limiting focus on the "exact" and the "concrete."

With C.S. Lewis we are concerned, I think, with more than a purely English peculiarity. When I hear him speak of the young pup which, in the middle of the hardship of being trained to cleanliness and order, would begin to have serious doubts, "supposing he were a theologian," about the goodness of man – then I am reminded of someone who speaks to a man named Callias in a street in Athens: "If your sons were foals or calves we would be able to find someone who would make them competent in the virtues appropriate to them. But they are human beings – what trainer do you intend to give them? Who is knowledgeable about human virtue?" These words are found in Plato's *Apologia*, and it is Socrates who speaks like this. Such robust, vigorous clarity of language can also be encountered, again and again, with other great writers. "If the will and the hand were two people, the hand would not commit sin; but the will would commit sin not just by its own doing – willing – but also by the action of the hand which it uses; but *one* person is the doer of both actions and will therefore be punished for both." These sentences, too, from the *Quaestiones disputatae* of St. Thomas, put the meaning completely within reach of the mind and the senses.

* * *

What follows is to be a short song of praise for such plainness, which seems to be an ever rarer phenomenon in philosophical books.

It can begin with a warning: *Be slow to trust, wherever this plainness is lacking; it is the seal of credibility.* Only he deserves to be believed who wants nothing for himself. But it is precisely in plainness of speech that selfless, free engagement with reality naturally comes to fruition and manifests itself. The same Goethe who, in seeing and "reading" things requires of himself silence and "complete renunciation of all pretention," preferred, in speaking, "the less impressive expression," so that only the clear character of the things themselves would become evident.

Of course, there can be extremely difficult statements which are comprehensible only to the few experts, which, however, are completely plain, while the "awful simplifiers" usually lack nothing so much as the selfless simplicity that looks away from itself.

Thus the distinction between true and false simplicity is at one and the same time a kind of "test" for the reader and listener. Here, too, we can find "pretention" and pomposity. Anyone who is prepared to be impressed by the fraudulent pomp of style and diction will, for this very reason, not have an eye for the insights that come with genuine simplicity.

* * *

There is not only "language" but also "terminology"; there is the artificial, constructed technical "term" which is settled on by agreement, alongside the more original, so to speak created "word" which has grown and has natural validity.

In praise of the books by C.S. Lewis the following must be said: they are almost free of "terminology," they are completely "language," and they show their simplicity also in this.

Here it is not a question of any sectarian campaign against "foreign words." Naturally it is simpler not to say "Fragmal" (as in a new German translation of Kierkegaard) but to say "Problem." However, everyone knows certain forms of "scientific" language which hardly have any connection with the everyday language we normally speak. Of course, not everyone will want to go as far as Erik Peterson, who – perhaps not altogether seriously – spoke of the disgusting, debasing language of science.

The issue raised by these comments is not first and foremost "intelligibility" and "readability," not the consideration, as it were, that a person dealing with words owes to the listener and reader; this question will also be addressed. *But what we are saying now is this: the word that has developed in human language contains more reality than do artificial terms.* That is the reverse side of that precision which is at the same time the specific advantage of the technical term. The notion "precise" refers to the technically produced cleanness of the smooth cut surface; with a view to achieving higher definition, the technical term isolates, as if by a surgical operation, the material in question and separates it out from all other content. In reality, however, there is no material content which can be clearly isolated and separated. The philosopher deals with this non-reduced reality – from which nothing is left out and cut away. This is what distinguishes him from the scientist who, rightly, limits himself to a particular aspect of reality and thereby addresses himself only to the specialist. But the incomprehensible always belongs as part of the material in question – and this is present in every word of natural speech, but not in the technical term. What the technical term aims to avoid, namely, that any kind of thought combinations lead beyond the limits of the fully illuminated area of meaning – precisely this is where the natural, historical language possesses an inexhaustible richness.

When medical people speak among themselves of "exitus" they are referring, with complete precision, to a clearly definable physiological fact. The word related to this technical term is: death. This word does not mean anything "precise" – nothing at all that is separated out. On the contrary, it refers to the non-reduced reality of what actually happens: the conclusion of the "way," of the status viatoris, whether it leads to salvation or otherwise; the loss of a father, a child, a lover; and also, of course, the process of extinction, of suffocation, of the heart stopping. (Because no one can be expected to confront the full reality of death on a daily basis, it is logical for the doctor to avoid it – precisely to protect the resoluteness of his healing operation – by not using the real name, the word, but the technical term.)

To say it again: the closer a writer remains to the natural speech of the people and the simpler his language is, the more it will be loaded with reality.

When Gabriel Marcel says, "We should keep to the normal, popular way of speaking which expresses experience in an infinitely more telling way than the pondered nomenclature of philosophical technical language," he is formulating a truth which the ancients took for granted. Not only Lao-tse, Plato, and Augustine, but also Aristotle and Thomas know – improbable as it may sound – no real special terminology. On the contrary, they have often themselves consciously and deliberately spoken of the force of that truth – as, for example, Thomas Aquinas, when he unfolds the richness of the word "with" [Greek: *pros.* DF] ("the Word was 'with' God") or the word "image," and in this he is investigating purely what people mean, explicitly or implicitly, when they say "with" or "image."

And C.S. Lewis stands in this same tradition. One only has to read the way he unfolds the meaning of the word "impossible."

* * *

The glory of the true teacher consists in his knowing how to look for and find the pupil where the pupil is; only in this way does being taught – and therefore also teaching – come about. But because every really philosophical question concerns everyone, the charisma precisely of the philosophical teacher is seen in the simplicity of his language.

The original medium of teaching is not the written word; the very great teachers have left nothing in writing. St. Thomas even dared to give as an example of this not only Pythagoras and Socrates, but Christ himself. But in the intimate intercourse of conferring, the flame of truth, as the seventy-year-old Plato expressed it in his Seventh Letter, is kindled in the soul unexpectedly, as if by a flying spark. Only the teacher who teaches face to face is able to be completely close to his listener and to take up his questions – which he has not expressed and which he is perhaps incapable of formulating.

Such directness of contact is not possible for the writer. However, he can come very close to it – by the simplicity of his language. It becomes clear that what is meant here is more than ordinary or even trivial "ease of understanding." What is meant, above all, is that inner dialog with the reader comes about and is maintained.

It has taken me a long time to understand what Socrates really means when, in his debates with the sophists, he continually rejects "speeches" and insists on "conferring": namely, that he opposes the partnerless speaking of the intellectual concerned with making an impression – the hopelessly cut-off "fifty-drachma"-monolog of the superior know-it-all. He opposes, therefore, a phenomenon which is well known in all ages.

The most pleasant books are those which neither ignore the reader nor bluff him, those where, in reading them, he is allowed to feel he is a partner in a peaceful conversation between gentlemen, enjoying the *cheerful respect* praised by Goethe.

* * *

We have given three-fold praise to simplicity of

language: as a guarantee of the credibility of the speaker; because of the richer objective fullness of what is said; because the dignity of the addressee, the partner, is preserved in a special way. One final comment now needs to be added.

The ancients said that philosophy is related to literature. While I was reading the book about suffering I came to a new realization of what this sentence means.

At first it sounds very strange to our ears, and perhaps we are little inclined to accept it as a meaningful statement. Or, even worse, we misunderstand it at the outset by taking philosophy to mean a kind of "conceptual literature." But the old meaning is: there is something which both philosophy and literature have in common: both, namely, have to do with the *mirandum*, with what is wonderful in the world. But that is a new and broad topic.

All that I am interested in saying here is that this original relationship must in fact sink into oblivion the further the language of philosophy removes itself from the language of literature. Of course, this does not mean that the philosopher should try to cultivate "poetic" language; but it does mean that the language of philosophy should not obscure the unfathomable ground of reality – on the contrary, it should give it expression in words, just as literature does in its own way. The language of philosophizing distances itself from the language of literature not by ceasing to be objective and sober but by losing its simplicity – I almost said, its innocence. No path leads from the technical term to the literary word; on the contrary, it obscures the fact that a path back and forth between philosophy and poetry already exists. Only the water of plain speech – the water that, because it is invisible itself, allows the beam of light to penetrate to the bottom – is capable of being turned into the wine of literature.

Boethius Poems,
Translated by Konrad Weiss

We are dealing with the prose, distributed over the Five
Books of the *Consolation of Philosophy*, which the approximately forty-five-year-old Boethius wrote while await-
ing his execution in prison in Pavia.

In the same period of five years in which this work
was written, between 525 and 530, two events occurred
which announced the end of an exhausted and the beginning of a new age. By order of the Christian Emperor
Justinian, the "Academy," Plato's school, which had
existed in Athens with this name for nine hundred years,
was closed. And the other event: Benedict of Nursia
founded the monastery of Monte Cassino, high above the
military roads of the great migrations. Antiquity, also
"Christian antiquity," was at an end. Augustine was
already a hundred years dead. It was the beginning of
centuries which, another thousand years later, people
would arrogantly call the "Middle Ages."

These dates not only situate Boethius historically, but
they also designate his inner fate. He has settled on the
narrow strip of no man's land which separates the eras –
which means that he is not completely and incontestably
at home either in the old or in the new.

It is true that in Boethius's life the two names are
linked which, down to the present, are able to conjure up
for us, in a unique way, the essence of antiquity: Rome
and Athens. One of the cities was the place of his birth;
and not only that: his family belonged to the old Roman
aristocracy. In the other city he did his philosophical
studies like many another Roman aristocrat before him.
One would think, after all this, that no stronger

rootedness in the soil of antiquity would be possible. But Boethius did not want to apply the energy of his heart to the mere preservation and administration of what was handed down. He became involved with what was new and different, that, first in the form of a barbarian invasion and then as a more openminded invading power, occupied the old imperial soil of Italy. He went to the court of Theodoric the Goth, where, even as a young man, he rose to high political office and dignity. In doing this, Boethius found himself, of course, in a position to succeed in preserving tradition in a way which would never have occurred to or have been achieved by those who were purely conservative.

On the other hand, the ambiguity of the middle position in which Boethius saw the task assigned to him is easy to see: he was the Roman at the German Prince's court, the "Greek" in the Christian domain, the Catholic Christian in the service of an Arian – and therefore heretical – regime. The mediator is always in danger of being misinterpreted and of coming under suspicion as the secret agent of an opposing power, as "collaborator" and traitor, as the one who belongs nowhere. So Boethius has undergone, right down to the threshold of our own century, the illogical fate of being seen as a non-Christian Neo-Platonist as well as a devout theologian and even a martyr, who, because of his faith, was put to death by Theodoric. This latter supposition has, in the meantime, been shown by historical research to be just as false as the former. But that the supposition can arise and be defended with evidence is significant. Above all, the death sentence which Boethius himself experienced as a howling injustice, seems to find its explanation in precisely that ambiguity: for Theodoric, who was in conflict with the

Roman emperor, would not the Roman at his own court be, by his very existence, suspected of high treason? Perhaps one can therefore assume that Boethius found his death precisely in the exercise of his office as mediator.

* * *

Anyone who today says the word "principle" is using a term coined by Boethius: it is one of many which point back to him. "Universal," "speculation," "accident," "define," "subject" – the same is true of all of these words. Boethius translated them from the Greek of Plato and Aristotle into Latin, into the language – learned also by the northern conquerors of the West, of the young West which was laying its foundations.

Translation is one of the recurring basic forms of mediation. Strictly speaking, the carrying over of a thought from one language into the other is an impossible business, because, of necessity, it changes the thought. On the other hand, what constitutes the achievement of the great translator is that he is able to reduce the change to a minimum.

Furthermore, it is not completely accurate to say that the translator "coins" a word. He sets up a relationship. The word *principium* has, of course, existed in Latin from time immemorial. But that the quintessence of all early philosophizing, the Greek word *arché* – in which the meaning "origin" is linked with the element of "ruling" – becomes continually represented by the equally ambiguous *principium*: precisely that is the work of the translator Boethius. To become aware of the accuracy of this translation, which omits nothing, we have only to think for a moment what German word we have to hand fully to capture the meaning of both *arché* and *principium* (Heidegger's accurate German translation "beherrschendes Woher" is more a definition than a translation).

The greatness of the translator Boethius is shown, above all, by the status of his subject. He could hardly have realized his plan to translate the main works both of Plato and of Aristotle even if, as the introductory poem of his Consolation book says, untimely death had not entered his ripening years. Thus he only managed some shorter writings of Aristotle. But it was through this translation of his (and the accompanying commentary) that Aristotle's presence was maintained in the Latin West at all. And Aristotle is not just any kind of author; he is this hardly imaginable thought-energy in whose field of radiation the basic things seem to become clear as if of themselves. When his complete works – almost seven hundred year after Boethius – after an adventurous course (through Latin translations of Arabic translations) become known in the universities [hohe Schulen. DF] of Italy and France, he brings about a revolution in which the West now finds its ultimate shape and identity.

* * *

In the handbooks of the history of philosophy Boethius is usually called the "first scholastic." The epithet refers to five little tracts about subjects of Christian theology which historians, after much debate, only a few decades ago finally established as writings of Boethius. One of these *opuscula sacra*, which has the Divine Trinity as its theme, does not contain one single sentence taken from

Sacred Scripture. An unheard of and momentous thing. Precisely this announces the advent of "scholasticism." The name "scholastic" is normally understood as a term that is neither particularly defined nor altogether flattering. But all serious attempts at definition agree on one point: it concerns an enormous organization of learning stretching over several centuries, in which the young peoples in the north and west of Europe sought to assimilate the immeasurable content of ancient and early-Christian tradition and, so to speak, to make it manageable – accessible to human thinking in its search for reasons. This is the common ground that links the Lombardian Anselm of Canterbury with the French Peter Abelard and both of them with the Swabian Albertus Magnus, the Hohenstaufen south Italian Thomas Aquinas, and the Oxford Franciscan Duns Scotus. But the earliest in the series is Boethius. He inaugurates it with the programmatic sentence which concludes one of his theological tracts: "Link, as much as you can, faith and reason." Étienne Gilson, of course, makes the comment that this formulation might possibly be found already in the writings of Augustine.

* * *

Boethius's greatest work was never planned by himself. It was forced out of him in a terrible way. With a single, completely unexpected blow, this existence, gloriously expanding in both intellectual and political spheres, was brought back to an intimate encounter with ultimate reality in a tiny cell.

The work of this writer and teacher was a result of his own deliberate intention and exerted an influence far into the coming centuries; it was sufficient to bring success and fulfillment – if we want to speak of such things – which are seldom accorded to an individual person. But this influence remained as good as anonymous. Only the erudite historian knows about it. The only product which, down the years, remains – and will remain – linked to the name Boethius is at the same time the only one which his own sketches in no way anticipated: the book on *The Consolation of Philosophy*.

This book can be read in very different ways. One can read it with a view to "recognizing," in its form, a Platonic type of dialog, an imitation of an early work of Aristotle, a prototype of Dante's *Vita nuova*, and, in its content, the teachings of Neoplatonism or the intellectual substance of the Stoics. Such reading is natural for the reader with an education in history and he sees himself attracted to it. But it is to be feared that it may, indeed, lead him to a number of useful observations but not to the point where he really hears the voice of Boethius. To achieve this latter one must be left alone with the book and direct the eyes and ears of the soul, without distraction, to what is directly being said. It emerges then that in the *Consolatio philosophiae* what happens is none other than that a man whose whole rich life substance has, without warning, been knocked out of his hand seeks to find out what is left. Nothing is more natural than for him to bring to bear all available knowledge – Platonist, Neo-Platonist, Aristotelian, Stoic. But he is not in the least concerned with erudite quotation from famous people nor with the creation of literature. What concerns him is simply a solid answer to the question, which is a matter of life and death, whether for him – yes or no? – the world and existence are meaningless. But not only this question is an eternal human question which one can encounter every day; also the answers which Plato or, for example, the Stoics have given are not at all something to be dismissed as historical. Who would want to maintain that we know "today" an answer that is quite simply new or even definitive? What would be the basis for our saying this? Here I hesitate. Who are the "we" in question? If "we Christians" are the ones meant, is not deeper and truer information accessible to us than is contained in all the wisdom of antiquity? This is exactly the basis for the supposition that Boethius could not have been a Christian: that the *Consolatio philosophiae* is silent about that Christian information. How is it to be explained that no express mention of Christ and no thought of the mystery of his Passion found entry into the reckoning of the man who needed consolation? Naturally, no one can provide an exact answer.

But could it not be that precisely this silence bears witness to the honesty and the completely unliterary character of Boethius' statement? There is in the *Consolatio*, the inner style of which, I think, is characterized by the most extreme lack of illusion ("Everyone has in himself something he does not know about as long as he has not tested it; but when he has tested it, he shudders") – there is in it a marvelous formulation that "nothing can be adorned by others' adornments." The meaning is this: what we possess only then becomes ours when, in the innermost region of our existence, it is transformed into ourselves; in the final analysis, what counts is what one "is," and not what one "has." Not every thought that a person has, and not everything that, as thought, is part of his treasure of knowledge already belongs to him as his own – no matter how much it is clear to the reflective reason or is affirmed in conscious acceptance. Understandably, here there are untold possibilities for the most sublime self-deception. A person could well have written a book about the Trinity – and then it emerges that, when it is a matter of life and death, he is not able to derive any benefit from this "knowledge." No one can anticipate the most extreme "test." But in it becomes apparent what belongs to us and what does not.

Could it not be, I say, that the "last Roman," although a profoundly upright Christian, found himself, "shuddering," thrown back on an interpretation of life in which the deepest consolation of the Christian mystery remained silent? Of course, immediately several things need to be noted: first, that the book of the *Consolation of Philosophy* could never have been written by a non-Christian. Not only would he have been incapable of thinking thoughts of providence or of defining eternity; he would not have been able to release, in such purity, the intransitory truth embedded in the rock of antique thought and bring it to light. Second, at no time has "faith" been readily at man's disposal. This fact cannot be done away with by things we take for granted in speaking and thinking about the mystery, but it can be consigned to oblivion.

* * *

The dialog which constitutes the content of the last book of Boethius is therefore not some kind of forced allegory. And neither of the partners between whom the conversation goes back and forth is an unreal invented figure. The one who speaks with the prisoner Boethius is the non-prisoner Boethius, his own *anima*, which is free because it keeps its gaze fixed on the divine guarantee of all meaning in the world – whereby, moreover, the Boethian definition both of spiritual freedom and of philosophy is almost literally rendered. The "lady philosophy" who enters the cell is, therefore, not an outline that declaims book wisdom; she is not at all "someone else"; she is the inner adversary of the prisoner himself. And the greatness of the *Consolatio philosophiae* lies in the fact that the tension in this conversation with the self is carried through without mitigation. The brutal reality of pain, of injustice, of being robbed defies every effort to discuss it away by abstract argumentation; but also the reality of an eternally intact order of things confronts the eye unyieldingly. Neither of the two partners spares the other, and neither reduces the other to silence.

The conversation begins in such a way that "philosophy" answers the unstoppable flow of lamentation from the prisoner by seeming to join in, to take it up and reinforce it. "Seeming" – for in this repetition there is a hardly perceptible new tone; it contains a suggestion of irony, a hint of what one might almost describe as derision. An understanding of the whole book depends, I think, on one's noticing this contrapuntal distance between the first poem and the second; this is what keeps the following discussion going and shows its real seriousness.

The theme of this discussion ("If God exists, where does evil come from? If God does not exist, where does good come from?") – this theme is of such a kind that even the most patient, the most independent effort not involving slavery to any vital need of an answer is not able to resolve it and reach any definitive result. But because the dialog is characterized both by the will to

227

clarify the situation as far as is possible for the capacity of the human mind and, at the same time, by the refusal to buy even the slightest element of information at the price of passing over a single difficulty – the *Consolatio philosophiae* cannot end in a stereotyped conclusion.

However, real consolation does come about: the man who is blinded by pain comes to see a new dimension of the world, and the man caught up in lamentations about his own loss becomes aware of the inexhaustible richness which consists in his belonging to that greater, more real reality.

* * *

It cannot be said that the work of Boethius has remained close to us. This is clear from the surprise we experience when we hear about the manifold influences he has exerted over a period of a thousand years.

The series of German translators of Boethius, the last of whom until now seems to have been Konrad Weiss, begins with the great Master of St. Gallen, Notker Labeo. A hundred years before him King Alfred had already translated the *Consolatio philosophiae* into English. We know of medieval translations into French and Greek; and in the Vatican Library there is even a Hebrew edition. – Between the eleventh and fifteenth century there were, in the West, apparently only a few important philosophers and theologians who did not write a Boethius commentary. – And the imitations of the book of the *Consolation of Philosophy* constitute an entire literary genre on their own. It is, indeed, astounding how many-voiced and lasting an echo was awakened by this book. Of course, it is hardly possible to check whether, after the Bible and the *Imitation of Christ*, any work of world literature has been more frequently copied, printed and commented upon. But we do have, for the period between 900 and the invention of the printing press, more than four hundred manuscripts of the *Consolatio philosophiae*. And it is a proven fact that just fifty years after the Gutenberg Bible there are already forty-three printed editions of Boethius's book.

* * *

What is special about the Boethius translation left us by Konrad Weiss is that it stoutly resists simple incorporation into this line of tradition. It was not really undertaken for the sake of Boethius. It was undertaken rather as an attempt to establish as exactly and emphatically as possible a fundamentally alien view of the world, which would then receive poetic expression as a contrast to his own conception. It seems, on the other hand, that precisely through this opposition such an unusual level of excellence in translation was achieved.

As his friends know, in his final years Konrad Weiss contemplated writing a play about Theodoric. Naturally, Boethius would have played an important part in this – as would his friend and pupil Cassiodorus, who likewise, as *magister officiorum*, held a high office at the court of the Gothic king. The plain historical facts radiate the excitement of this configuration: the ruler of a Germanic tribe who grew up as a hostage in Byzantium and became a convert to Arian Christianity and the most powerful ruler of his age as well as a forerunner of the German Emperors; the Roman Christian, Boethius, with his deep roots in the Greek intellectual tradition, who sought direct contact with the emerging powers and was thereby destroyed; finally, Cassiodorus, also a Roman but of Syrian extraction, who suddenly gives up a successful political career and then, in more than thirty years of monastic seclusion strives in his own way to achieve Boethius's goal. – But, of course, the dramatic work Konrad Weiss was planning would not have been, as he said himself, "merely a matter of illustration." There are no available notes by the writer that give more details about his plan. Yet he did, on several occasions – for example, in some important letters, copies of which are found in his unpublished works – say how the characters, above all of Theodoric and Boethius, began to take shape, "with there being no possibility of an understanding between them, and that the death (of Boethius), even though caused politically, was intrinsically linked with circumstances of the period." At the same time, contrary to all humanistic thinking, not Theodoric but Boethius is seen as the foreigner. Again and again, wherever Konrad Weiss describes the intellectual position of the king of the Goths he suddenly says "we" instead of "Theodoric." He is always seen as superior, whereas Boethius is seen as someone who lacks something important: "The 'last of the Romans' lacks historical awareness of what the German, in the context of the migrations, must reckon with as if blindly."

Anyone with even a scanty knowledge of Konrad Weiss's work knows that "blindness" is one of the fundamental words he uses in attempting to define the essence of historical experience. What he means is "the pure trust" kindled by the contemplation of the "historical Gethsemane" that is not accessible to the reckoning power of the *ratio*. This phrase ("historical

Gethsemane"), taken from Vincent van Gogh, recurs in Konrad Weiss's work in varying forms. It is certainly clear that for the poet the contrasting of Theodoric with Boethius is not first and foremost an "historical" problem in the narrow sense, although he considers it an obvious requirement to know the scholarly literature about his subject. It is a question of trying to find an answer to the question he has pondered throughout his life: whether and how it is possible, from the immediacy of experience, to glimpse the salutary meaning of history.

And so Boethius appears – "in the elegiac contemplation of the stars and the unmistakable regularity of the movements of the cosmos" – as the "classical" man whose limit consists precisely in his aim to avoid blindness, to see and understand, to see the clear shape of things. "Our" way, by contrast, is "more like hearing," he says. One can ask what can be accessible to such blind hearing that is also not visible to the eye of the soul. The answer is: that which never reveals itself, the message from out of inaccessible light, the Pentecostal outpouring of the Spirit's breath; and also the dark sounds of fate as time moves into the future. A sentence like the following that relates to the first months of the last World War: "Time is like the water one hears flowing and does not know where it flows; and one thinks it is flowing and roaring at a great height" – this sentence, which, by the way, is a quotation from Friedrich von Spee, is fully in accord with the basic notion under discussion here. – The humanism of Boethius is seen as essentially unaware that the world is more than something which can be exhaustively looked at and expressed. His humanism does not see the "gap," the "lack," the "fundamental negative aspect" [Ingrund. DF] in the structure of history. Nor does it see that, through all the pain of this wound, a healing is glimpsed which infinitely and inexpressibly transcends all positivity. Konrad Weiss cannot be accused of basing his interpretation, as happens in classicism, on a simplified image of "ancient" man. On the contrary, in one of the letters referred to, he contrasts the "heaviness of the ancient *pondus*" he finds in Boethius with the crystalline renaissance clarity of the self-assured *ratio*. However, as he says, the tomb of Theodoric in Ravenna has a "much darker seriousness . . . than it was possible for the ancient *anima* to grasp. Antiquity certainly had immense suffering and immense pathos, but it did not have that disturbing simplicity that 'says nothing,' as, for instance, in the case of Shakespeare's Cordelia."

Such are the things that Konrad Weiss intended to deal with in the introduction to his translation of the poems of Boethius. He did not write it. The text I have in my possession bears the date 21 September 1939. Three months later, on 4 January 1940, Konrad Weiss died, a few months before his sixtieth birthday.

This writer – deliberately so un-Latin in his outlook – by becoming involved with the "hardship," as he calls it, of translating as accurately as possible the verse of this "last of the Romans"; by being able to tauten the string of his bow to overcome resistance and distance and to shoot off the last remaining arrow in his quiver, produced an *opusculum* in which things which I feel are irreconcilable are felicitously combined: the architectural clarity of Latin concepts and the vivid verbal imagery originating from pre-Lutheran German.

The Good Publisher
A birthday greeting for Jakob Hegner

What it takes to make a good author, dear Herr Hegner, you outlined for me during the interval between my first and second book. It was one early morning in Leipzig at a roughly-hewn table in a cheerless Greek pub you had just discovered in the furrier's district. On the handwritten wine list some surprising things were drawn. This circumstance is probably the reason why I have almost completely forgotten the details of your instruction. But I still know how much you insisted that a good author must above all be lively, by which you did not at all mean special peculiarities of expression but, to my surprise, the simple fact that the author must be still alive. (In this regard there are clearly quite different views. Just now, for example, my English translator has written to me that in future he will only become involved with dead authors.) Of course, what *you* meant in speaking of a "good" author was: "good" for the publisher!

One can also turn the tables and ask what makes a good publisher, thereby meaning: "good" for the author! – Here a variety of things could be mentioned. And I see the worry beginning to show in your eyes that I might belabor a defenseless man with a catalog of virtues. No! – although I like the idea of taking a closer look at the particular way a publisher is prudent, just, and courageous, whatever form that might take. What the author, the one who produces the manuscript, expects first and foremost from the publisher is something much less exalted. It is simply this: *that it happens quickly!* As soon as the manuscript is sent off to the publisher (yes, whether it is *the* publisher is precisely what is in question!) – from that moment the author devotes himself ardently to the activity of waiting. That should not be something too hard to understand. And a "good" publisher must really be capable of knowing the deadly effect of the measured communication: "We gratefully confirm receipt of your manuscript. We will send it on to our editorial department. Assuming that . . ." and so on. What a relief when finally, after the author has made several inquiries, the letter comes which begins with very special praise of the unusually interesting manuscript – which, however, for purely extraneous reasons unfortunately cannot be taken on at the present moment and is being returned herewith.

I had spent the summer of 1934 playing such cruel games, repeated half a dozen times, when I finally hit on the desperate idea of sending my manuscript on "The Meaning of Courage" – which I was already calling my "boomerang" – to the publisher of Bernanos, Claudel and Haecker. Three days later I was thinking of going for a bike ride to the Lahn. Fortunately, an enormous storm delayed my departure, so that I was still at home to receive your first letter to me on 4 September 1934. The first sentence was the highly improbable statement that you had received my manuscript the previous evening and had "that very evening and in the early hours of the following morning completed reading it" and had made up your mind to print the little book. The next day I rode to the Lahn – and found in Marburg your second letter which contained the even more improbable sentence: "I could publish two such books a year written by you!" What could be more natural than that, as I rode through the summer river valley, I contemplated a plan to write a book about hope! – On my return, the proofs of the

"Courage" book already lay on the table. And seven weeks after your first letter, when I was innocently rummaging through books in a bookshop, I chanced on the finished book with its bright blue linen cover. It was pure magic. This report is the unvarnished truth. But perhaps you have forgotten?

A young author needs such a publisher. One simply needs, when one has sent a sample chapter, to have, by return of mail the answer that says: it is "captivatingly" written. I did then find out later how much and how often you like to use this favorite expression of yours. But at the time I was so encouraged by it that, in a wonderful winter, I was able to write down the remaining chapters on hope in one sitting, as it were. Moreover, also the *opusculum* "On Hope" appeared not much more than two months after the manuscript was handed in – on the very day of my wedding.

It is with joy, and to thank you, that I remind you – and also myself – of this beginning: the little books on the image of man, which have become a part of my real work, would perhaps never have come about – without the "good" publisher!

Late Apology to Rudolf Alexander Schröder

I entertain the silent and perhaps too audacious hope that these somewhat personal lines will not be seen by the poet Rudolf Alexander Schröder – although they are meant as homage, which of course has been ventured late enough, but still on time for the celebration of his seventy-fifth birthday.

It began badly enough, with a discord. As young people, around 1900, we read Theodor Haecker with enthusiasm, for he appealed to us above all as a polemicist. This was perhaps understandable; but it was not good. It is not healthy for a young mind to contemplate the world in a spirit of irony and satire. – An object of such witty destruction was, in Haecker's Virgil book, a line from the *Aeneid* translation by "Herrn" Rudolf Alexander Schröder. I am still today of the opinion that this verse is not one of the poet's most successful. But I think the passage which is a blemish on Haecker's beautiful book is even worse. Incidentally, it has been omitted from the later edition. And Haecker, who, as he says himself, was in his early years burning with impatience, confessed in the "Day and Night Books" how much he realizes that pure polemicism is unfruitful, vain, and frustrating, and how much he "regrets" it.

For us, at that time, access to the work of R.A. Schröder was in this way, if not blocked, then at least hindered. I remember well the efforts of a friend to acquaint me with Schröder's translation of the *Iliad*. I was moved when I heard the "silver ring" of these verses which my friend was able to extol with his lovely enthusiasm; however, my admiration, passing by the translator, went directly to Homer himself. And when, later, I found in

Felix Timmerman's "Pallieter" two masterly poems by Guido Gezelle, I almost missed the footnote referring to the name of the translator as R.A. Schröder.

I achieved real attention, uninhibited listening, only when, on a business trip to Berlin in 1942 or 1943, I visited Peter Suhrkamp in his tower of the "Zuschauer" and he gave me a printed sheet from a proof copy of Schröder's poems to take with me. Then, in a rather noisy train for holiday-makers, I read for the first time with really open eyes and without inhibition the "Ballad of the Wayfarer," the first parts of which have since then belonged to my favorite poems.

> Don't touch me; – it's not me anymore
> – Look rather, as if by chance
> Into the bright variety of things.
> I broke bread, sat by the fire
> And held you all for sweet and worthy:
> It seems to me that that is gone –

I only need to say these verses to myself and the world changes; I see, behind the foreground confusion, the very simple structure of man's fate in death, a quite clear and not at all hopeless structure. Such power of reverie, such ability to reveal the hidden foundation of things are proof of a great and true poem.

But if I were asked what I think is R.A. Schröder's most beautiful poem, the most poetic one, I would, without hesitation, name the two short-line strophes "Selig Gesicht" written when he was about fifty years old. These verses have a fundamentally original sound, they are an overpowering exclamation of astonishment that goes through the soul like a violent wave – in which for the first time the earliest contours of the emerging crystal, the form contained in rhyme and image, begins to emerge:

> Blessed face,
> Always the one
> Blessed face
> Over the world,
> Behind the world,
> Come and appear,
> Rose of the meadow,
> Star in the sky.
>
> That I may see you,
> In blue above me
> Over the world,
> Behind the world,
> That I may die
> Seeing but you
> Rose of the meadow
> Star in the sky.

One evening when I had praised this poem and then was still not able, with full certainty, to quote it from memory and reached for the "Hundred Spiritual Poems" of my friend – *the* hundred poems which R.A. Schröder himself had recently selected, probably as the ones which spoke to him the most, I was surprised to find that "Selig Gesicht" was not in the selection and that therefore this delightful poem had not found grace with its author.

For which reason this little plea closes in the hope that it may perhaps not have been altogether superfluous.

"Important Support and Advancement through a Single Word"
For Romano Guardini on his 70th birthday

You cannot know, revered Romano Guardini, how often I sat at your feet from the time I was sixteen years old until about my twenty-third year – first at Rothenfels on the Main and later in the lecture rooms and seminar of the Berlin University. You are not able to know it because for those seven years I remained a consistently silent listener, looking with envious respect at the circle of those who ventured to speak with you so naturally about Kierkegaard, Dostoevsky or about any other of the many "problems" which exercised us. Only much later, after I had myself produced some *opuscula*, did we meet for the first time in a mutual encounter. But if the one who had listened to you so intently has remained unrecognizable, I am, for my part – as I am surprised to realize at this very moment – no longer able to say in detail what we really spoke about on that occasion. I hope this observation does not grieve you. It is precisely this fact that indicates to me how intensely I took your words to heart: they went down so deep within me that, if things happened as they should, one day an insight of my own would come about, so that indications of its origin would be dissolved in this process of assimilation and lost. I think you would agree with me: the teacher teaches most successfully when the listener acquires the teaching as his own – in such a way that he forgets its origin and thereby also the teacher. I must be completely mistaken if I did not hear for the first time from your mouth the superb saying: "Do not be concerned about Socrates; be concerned about the truth."

But today I would like to speak of a moment that, although it happened more than thirty years ago, remains very clear in my memory. It is a single sentence from a talk in the Knights Hall in Rothenfels, which I think you had improvised, on Goethe's birthday – 28 August – in 1924. It is a single sentence which, with a stroke, changed my whole world. The Goethean formulation in the above title expresses very exactly what I, too, experienced: important support and advancement.

I wonder whether we ever again receive knowledge which penetrates into the depths of our soul as when, at twenty years of age, we listen to the words of a beloved and revered teacher. That hour, of course, was blessed in a special way by all good spirits; you yourself later spoke of that Goethe celebration as of something particularly successful.

Furthermore, there was discussion not only of Goethe but also of Thomas Aquinas and of what they both had in common: the "classical" spirit. At that time I had read my way, with enthusiasm, into the *Summa theologica*, especially the second part which contains the fundamentals of ethical teaching about life. I had already formed the plan of describing a particular fundamental idea of this teaching which dealt with the rightness of man in his existence, and of interpreting this in a work of my own. My professors were skeptical. They thought I should limit myself to a less far-reaching topic, preferably an historical theme which could be completed within a predictable time frame. But I remained stubborn. I wanted to grasp the point that seemed extremely important to me and which I had not yet quite managed to take hold of; I wanted this crystalline structure which I saw, still very unclearly –

vaguely sensed rather than saw – forming out of the fluidity, not to slip from my grasp and from sight. And what happened now when I heard you speak, no, when I heard this one sentence, was this: in a flash the crystal took on a clear shape!

The actual wording of this sentence – I must again confess – is, despite everything, no longer there: I could not dredge it up from my memory. And I don't have to hand the booklet "Schildgenosse" with its report about those Rothenfels days. But what the sentence meant and what I will never forget is the following: all obligation is grounded in being; the good is what corresponds to reality. Whoever wants to know and do what is good must direct his gaze to the objective world of being; not to his own "convictions," not to "conscience," not to "values," not to the "ideals" and "models" he has chosen. He must forget about his own involvement and look at reality.

Incidentally, these formulations are quotations, self-quotations. They are the sentences with which my first work begins, which I was now enabled to write – "through a single word" from you.

I am adding here an epilog, a kind of coda: how is it that, in this country, when one writes down a personal reminiscence like this, one has to overcome a certain resistance within oneself, as if one were doing something embarrassing, unobjective, or at least something superfluous? "In another country" we don't seem to sense this inhibition. When I recently received a bibliographical and biographical handbook sent to me from America, I found to my (for a moment) almost indignant surprise this whole story narrated: "The plan to his first book was born during a lecture on Goethe and Thomas Aquinas given by Romano Guardini at the Jugendburg Rothenfels on Main in 1924; the lecture was entitled 'About Classical Spirit.'" From this we can see that "over there" I must have spontaneously related what "here" I can only write with hesitation.

"Where Do We Stand Today?"

This very question is already something problematic. Provided it cannot be answered satisfactorily by reference, let us say, to the state of technology, to the flight to the cities or the end of white colonial domination; provided the question, as one suspects, refers to the totality of things, it conjures up – in the first instance –a journey, the greater or lesser part of which has already been traveled: do we "stand" at the beginning or perhaps already at the end? It is known that there are a number of contradictory answers to this question. One of them says we are already in fact approaching the "evening," whereas, on the other hand, we are assured that the human race is biologically still very young and is currently only experiencing the earliest hours of the morning. But both views, long since equally discussed and played off one against the other, can, of course, only have meaning if our road is analogous to the course of the day or a human lifespan. They presuppose that we know the entire stretch of the way more or less exactly. But precisely this is not the case. The scale on which the distance of our present position can be subtracted and gauged, both from the point Alpha and, above all, from the point Omega, is simply unknown to us.

Secondly, who is meant by this "we"? All who belong to world-wide European history? Humanity as a whole? The individual person? This latter, too, could give the question a legitimate meaning. And anyone who would answer this question, saying that "we," the individual human beings, "today" and in any conceivable present moment do not "stand" far away from death, from an event, therefore, that no one knows inwardly – such a person might not be far wrong. Of course, it would have to be added that we are at the same time *"viatores"* on an entirely different route on which the steps taken are by their fundamental nature decisions; that, furthermore, death, while certainly meaning the conclusion of this journey, does not necessarily mean arriving at our goal; and that the milestones of this journey remain obscured from everyone's vision; for which reason no one is in a position to say "where we stand today." I do not make the mistake of thinking that such thoughts are, in an almost annoying way, missing the point of the initial question. However, I would like to insist that largely there is no historical occurrence at the foundation of which the two aspects of this journeying of the single human individual are not in play. It also seems to me somewhat important not to forget the shape of the thought that is emerging here: namely, that the "ending of the journey" and "arriving at the goal" are not necessarily the same thing; or, in other words, that the end can also take the shape of missing the target.

If, therefore, the question about where we stand at present is clearly related to the worldwide society of European civilization, insofar as its fate seems to be becoming more and more identical with that of humanity as a whole, then, *thirdly*, we have to consider that, of course, we are not really "standing" at all. This journey on which we find ourselves is of such a kind that there is not only no stopping place but that rather the speed of the journey is constantly increasing. Can the crew of a space missile meaningfully ask: Where do we "stand" today?

These reservations and concerns drastically reduce the claim that could be made in any attempt to diagnose the present time. Today, in such an attempt, the fact that man has penetrated into interplanetary space is usually the first thing to be mentioned. This is undoubtedly appropriate, not least because both world powers are equally concerned. But a lot is to be said for the supposition that through this primarily technical fact the fundamental reality of existence is, deep down, as little affected and changed as it is by the extension of the other human fields of action with which we have already become acquainted. Here we are not refusing to respect this achievement or denying that, on the whole, it documents a constant and accelerated progress in harnessing the forces of the universe.

Of course, progress of this kind has always had the character of "chance." But part of the concept of "chance" is that it can be used, come into our awareness; and also be missed, wasted, and used destructively. Whenever the attempt is made to name the elements of the present situation, this ambivalence of all human achievements, which is unavoidable like freedom itself, is constantly revealed, showing sometimes the positive and sometimes more clearly the negative possibility, and sometimes, in a confusing way, both at the same time. We know only too well that this latter applies, to a special degree, to the model case of the atomic energy now at our disposal, with regard to which no one is in a position to say whether the danger of physical destruction and of political abuse can be offset – or not – by the equally undoubted possibility of its meaningful use.

But in this embarrassment a recurring structure is intimated. For example, research into human body-soul reality has given us unprecedented means of healing (through surgery, medicine, psychotherapy); but also:

never have there been such possibilities of violent dehumanizing, slavery, abduction, and of people being led astray by other people. Never before has the total substance of human wisdom been so effortlessly available to the individual as it is today; but never before has the individual, on the basis of this same chance, been so much in danger of seeing his own culture and that of others as "purely historical" and thereby losing both. Never has the unity of the natural world been evinced with such compelling scientific evidence; but also, by the same token, never has the negation of the dignity of the human spirit had such powerful arguments at its disposal.

But since the question "where do we stand today?" is obviously looking to the future, who will, given such ambivalence, venture to answer it? Even if we knew whether the human race is "young" or "old" (something about which nothing at all can be said), we would still not know whether it will attain its "natural" age or not. No one can be an exempted from this fundamental ignorance.

This is the point to make a comment about the special position of the Christian. Not that the Christian could give a full answer – by no means.

As is well known, a Christian is above all defined by his or her acceptance – as inviolable truth – of information about humanity and the world which is not accessible by natural means. (I am speaking about Christianity as a fact, without discussing the question whether it is right to be a Christian.) Some of those pieces of information concern the end of human history – which means that anyone who, as a Christian, reflects on the course of history cannot avoid including consideration of these pieces of information. In no way do they put the

Christian in a position to form a concrete idea of the final "outcome." Yet what is offered him here is not insignificant. What is said, amongst other things, is that the end of our finite history will not be simply identical with the "victory" of reason, of the good, of justice or even of Christianity and the Church; the last epoch directly preceding the transformation of the temporal order as a whole will, on the contrary – to put it briefly – be characterized by some sort of pseudo order embracing the whole planet and sustained by the rule of force.

Nothing is surer than that this prophetic vision of the end will encourage and even evoke a thousand misunderstandings both from non-Christians and Christians alike. This is not the place to discuss them. Still, it should be clear that one cannot deal properly with the Christian idea of history by declaring it to be "pessimistic," "fatalistic," or "quietist." It involves no need, for instance, to see the present as the "end of time." As we know, a sober analyst like Alexander Rüstow recently referred to it as a "purely empirically verifiable fact" that our situation is "eschatological in the fullest apocalyptic sense of the word." And Reinhold Schneider, who for the whole of his life sought knowledge of the hidden forces at work in our history, noted shortly before his death that he was convinced that we were near the end of history: "Our time is the interval between the end of the Reich and the last hand movement of the clock." Those are unquestionably statements of considerable seriousness and weight and many people will agree unreservedly. However, in defense against a not unusual but unjustified simplification, it must be said: a person can be quite convinced of the truth of the apocalyptic prophecy and yet at the same time think that these diagnoses of the present are false.

On the other hand, anyone who, as a Christian, reckons on a catastrophic end of history caused from within will not be surprised by these predictions. This constitutes the superiority which distinguishes the Christian from, for example, the liberal believer in progress who would inevitably be plunged into an abyss of bewilderment by the appearance of a criminal regime of force which would ("in the middle of the twentieth century!") terrorize whole nations. This advantage is based on the greater ability to sniff the apocalyptic which is radiated by certain historical manifestations. Things like the growing power, all over the world, of purposely produced seeming realities (in business advertising and "entertainment" as well as in political propaganda); the progressive stifling of natural reality by the artificial; the increasingly banal treatment of Eros and death, the forces which move us profoundly; the provision of an immense armory of instruments for manipulating masses of people which, for the time being, seems meant for no other purpose than to satisfy public curiosity and to relieve boredom – such manifestations reveal to the gaze which is prepared by that eschatological knowledge a secret symbol which necessarily escapes purely positivistic assessment.

Of course, these predictions contain no statement about how far they are from, or how close they are to, the event in question. The insight that has resulted, which should perhaps only be called a premonition (a supposition, a worry), does not immediately enable a more precise, or even any answer at all – to the question about where we presently "stand." It could, indeed, more readily make a person see the most human way to function in history as possibly just "mending" – doing something provisional and makeshift. He will apply the energy of his heart to exploiting the chances opened up to us today to achieve knowledge of the world as well as to give shape to the world and to one's own personality – filled with a hope that looks beyond this historical world before our eyes and yet affirms it and keeps it in view. Of course, with regard to the question "where do we stand today," the Christian, precisely because affected by the apocalyptic prophecy, will be inclined simply to abstain from giving an answer.

The attitude which is contrary to such abstention is sufficiently well known. I am referring to the largely threatening claim that not only says we have "scientific" knowledge of the overall plan of human history but also that we, as the solely responsible organ of world reason, are in the process of putting the plan into practice by our own efforts. Here there is, quite logically, not the slightest hesitation to provide information about "where we stand today." On the contrary, nowhere in the world is such unwavering certainty to be encountered. And again, corresponding to this lack of theoretical problems, there is the dogmatic claim to adherence imposed by force in political praxis.

That could, and should, be enough to arouse mistrust – not only against this particular answer, but against *every* attempt to give absolute definition to the goal of a *finished* humanity and from there to establish our present position.

At any rate, we should be under no illusion: the alluring power of the communist thesis is based on the fact that, in contradiction to all its programmatic insistence, it reaches out beyond the world we experience empirically and, moreover, even includes an historical prophecy –

not only in the shape of a utopia but also in the shape of a false, spurious theology. Such a claim can, naturally, not be refuted with the methods of "science," whether of sociology or of political science. A pseudo theology can only be defeated by a true theology. Here the discussion moves sharply and inevitably towards an horizon where thought is unable to predict and to limit. But to have the discussion in a more modest way is a fruitless undertaking. Only when faced with this horizon does that authority come into view from which alone we can be prepared to accept information about ourselves which is all-embracing and which alone can bring us to the point that "we are willing" *not* to know where human history is heading, and consequently, not to know "where we stand today."

Notes

To avoid encumbering this volume with a large apparatus of footnotes I have not quoted individual sources of material and quotations. These can be found in the first publication of each of the contributions.

"Tradition in the changing world" (Tradition in der sich wandelnden Welt). A lecture on the "Deutschen Hüttentag 1960" in Düsseldorf, 4 November 1960, on the occasion of the centenary celebration of the Verein Deutscher Eisenhüttenleute. First appeared in "Stahl und Eisen"; 80 (1960) number 25.

"What is meant by the 'Christian West'?" (Was heisst "Christliches Abendland"?) Slightly revised text of a radio talk (Norddeutscher Rundfunk); appeared in the collection "Europa. Vermächtnis und Verpflichtung," edited by Hansgeorg Loebel, Frankfurt am Main, 1957.

"What is, in truth, worth preserving" (Über das in Wahrheit Bewahrenswerte). Speech at the official opening of the Gymnasium Paulinum in Münster/Westphalia 26 June 1959.

"Death and Immortality" (Tod und Unsterblichkeit). Appeared in *Festschrift für Alois Dempf*; *Philosophisches Jahrbuch*, number 68, Munich 1960.

"Immortality – a non-Christian idea?" (Unsterblichkeit – eine nicht-christliche Vorstellung?) Lecture to an ecumenical study group of Evangelical and Catholic theologians (Spring 1959). Appeared in *Catholica*,

Vierteljahresschrift für Kontroverstheologie, number 13, Münster 1959.

"Doing and Signifying" (Bewirken und Bedeuten). Slightly abridged text of television lecture July 1960 on the occasion of the Eucharistic Congress in Munich. Appeared in the journal *Hochland*, 52/6.

"Consecration of the World" (Heiligung der Welt). Answer to a questionnaire circulated by the journal *Wort und Wahrheit*, Freiburg, the findings of which were published in the 1958 number.

"Life of the Spirit" (Leben des Geistes). A leader article appearing in the *Frankfurter Allgemeine Zeitung* at Pentecost 1955.

"The Theory of Virtues as Statement about Man" (Tugendlehre als Aussage über den Menschen). An entry printed in *Handbuch theologischer Grundbegriffe*, ed. Heinrich Fries, Munich 1962/63.

"Hope – of What?" (Hoffnung – auf was?). A leader article in the *Frankfurter Allgemeine Zeitung*, Easter 1957.

"The Hidden Nature of Hope and Despair" (Die Verborgenheit von Hoffnung und Verzweiflung). Lecture at the Fourth International Congress for Peace and Christian Culture in Florence 1955. Appeared in *Wort und Wahrheit*, number 10, Freiburg-Vienna 1955.

"The Seed Requires Soil" (Der Same bedarf des Erdreichs). On the occasion of the 10th anniversary of 20

July 1944. Appeared in several German newspapers. Reprinted in *Bekenntnis und Verpflichtung. Reden und Aufsätze zur zehnjährigen Wiederkehr des 20 July 1944,* Stuttgart 1955.

"Religion and Freedom" (Religion und Freiheit). Contribution to discussion at the Berlin "Congress for cultural freedom." Appeared in the journal *Hochland,* 53 (1960), Munich. The English version appeared in the congress proceedings as "History and Hope. Progress in Freedom," edited by K.A. Jelenski, London, 1962.

"Leisure and Human Existence" (Musse und menschliche Existenz). Text of a radio talk (Radio Bremen); appeared in the journal "Universitas," Stuttgart 1959.

"The Necessary But Also Impossible Business of Teaching" (Über das zugleich notwendige und unmögliche Geschäft des Lehrens). Speech on the occasion of the official opening of the Aula Building of the Pedagogical Institute Münster/Westphalia on 22 November 1958.

"On Plato's Concept of Philosophy" (Über den Philosophie-Begriff Platons). Lecture for the "Jahresfeier" of the North-Rhine-Westphalian "Arbeitsgemeinschaft für Forschung" in the Conference Room of the Düsseldorf Landtag, May 1955. Appeared in the series "Arbeitsgemeinschaft für Forschung des Landes Nordrhein-Westfalen," Cologne-Opladen 1955. The first sentence is a reference to the fact that on such festive occasions the members of the study group wore professorial garb.

"The equitable interpretation" ("Billigkeit" in der Interpretation). Appeared in "Karl-Arnold-Festschrift," Cologne-Opladen 1955.

"Platonic Figures" (Platonische Figuren). Both sketches are part of a series of radio lectures; appeared in *Neue Deutsche Hefte*, 1954 and 1955.

"Conversation as the place of truth" (Das Gespräch als Ort der Wahrheit). Appeared in "Der Brief," *Mitteilungsblatt der Pädagogischen Akademie Essen*, Christmas 1955.

"On Plainness of Language in Philosophy" (Über die Schlichtheit der Sprache in der Philosophie). Epilogue to C.S. Lewis "On Suffering." Translated by Hildegard and Josef Pieper. Verlag Jakob Hegner, Cologne, 1954.

"Boethius Poems, translated by Konrad Weiss" (Boethius-Gedichte, translated by Konrad Weiss). Epilog to the Latin-German edition ("Konrad Weiss, Die Gedichte aus der Tröstung der Philosophie des Boethius") which appeared as "Tausenddruck II," Suhrkamp, Berlin-Frankfurt am Main 1956. Individual sections have been used, more or less word for word, in the Boethius chapter of my "Scholastik" book, Munich 1960.

"The Good Publisher" (Über den guten Verleger). Appeared in the Hamburg weekly "Die Zeit" as well as in the *Festschrift zum 70. Geburtstag von Jakob Hegner*, 25 February, 1952.

Late apology to Rudolf Alexander Schröder (Späte Abbitte an Rudolf Alexander Schröder). Appeared in "Die Zeit," Hamburg, 26 January 1953.

"Support and advancement through a single word" (Bedeutende Fördernis durch ein einziges Wort). Appeared in "Die Zeit," Hamburg, for the 70th birthday of Romano Guardini, 17 February 1955.

"Where do we stand today?" (Wo stehen wir heute?). Appeared in a volume of essays under the same title, edited by H.W. Bähr, Gütersloh 1960. The title of the contribution there is: "Being on the Way" (Auf dem Wege sein).

Index of Names